Presbyterian Worship
Questions and Answers

Presbyterian Worship
Questions and Answers

David Gambrell

WESTMINSTER
JOHN KNOX PRESS
LOUISVILLE • KENTUCKY

First edition
Published by Westminster John Knox Press
Louisville, Kentucky

19 20 21 22 23 24 25 26 27 28—10 9 8 7 6 5 4 3 2 1

Scripture quotations from the New Revised Standard Version of the Bible are copyright © 1989 by the Division of Christian Education of the National Council of the Churches of Christ in the U.S.A. and are used by permission.

Question 12 is adapted from David Gambrell, "Seven Ways to Make Worship More Seeker-Friendly," *Presbyterians Today* 104, no. 10 (November 2014): 48.

Book design by Sharon Adams and Allison Taylor
Cover design by Allison Taylor

Library of Congress Cataloging-in-Publication Data is on file at the Library of Congress, Washington, DC.

ISBN-13: 9780664263973

To my daughters, Miriam and Noa,
whose questions are an inspiration, challenge, and delight.

Contents

Acknowledgments

I am indebted to the many teachers, colleagues, and friends who have fostered my own liturgical formation and have encouraged me to wrestle with these questions—particularly Ron Anderson, Chip Andrus, Cláudio Carvalhaes, Harold Daniels, Ruth Duck, Teresa Eisenlohr, Stan Hall, David Hogue, Myungsil Kim, Kim Long, Bill McConnell, Martha Moore-Keish, Gail Ramshaw, Joe Small, and Charles Wiley. I am grateful for the wisdom and patience of my editor, David Maxwell. And I cherish the love and support of my spouse, Sara Gambrell.

Introduction

Beginning in the sixteenth century, Protestant Reformers used catechisms—little books of questions and answers—to teach the basics of Christian faith, life, and worship. One of those documents, the 1647 Westminster Shorter Catechism, has been especially influential for generations of Presbyterians. It begins with this deceptively simple question: "What is the chief end of man?" (*Book of Confessions*, 7.001)—or to update the language—What is the meaning of human life?

Answer: To glorify and enjoy God forever. That's our highest goal, our deepest longing, our greatest delight. And that's exactly what Christian worship is all about: glorifying and enjoying God, now and forever. We can glorify and enjoy God in many ways—at work, at play, through service and study, with family and friends, and in personal prayer. But the clearest example comes in Christian worship, when the people of God are gathered in the presence of Jesus Christ and the power of the Holy Spirit. This is where we come to know the glory of God and the purpose of the life that God has given us. Of course, our services of worship don't always measure up to this lofty goal. The church—and its worship—are "always being reformed" (*semper reformanda*) according to God's Word and Spirit.

This is a book of questions and answers, like those Reformed catechisms. It reflects more than a decade of experience working in the national offices of the Presbyterian Church (U.S.A.), where I answer questions about worship almost every day. Indeed, the questions in this book are inspired by those real-life e-mails, phone calls, and conversations. As in those exchanges, I always try to use these questions as opportunities for deeper reflection on worship and discipleship. My hope is that readers will find much practical guidance in these pages—but more importantly, that they will be able to practice thinking theologically about worship, developing new questions and answers of their own.

This book may be used in a variety of ways—it might be read section by section or used as a reference for particular questions, a resource for worship committees, a study for sessions seeking to renew or reform the congregation's worship, or in the training of pastors, musicians, and other worship leaders. It is not necessary to read the questions in order. The short format of each answer might be used as a prompt for further discussion or reflection around a particular topic. A glossary in the back offers brief definitions of key terms.

This book includes numerous references to other books. As Presbyterians, our ultimate authority on worship is the Bible, as it reveals the Word of God made flesh in Jesus Christ; quotations from Scripture and other biblical references are noted in parentheses. The creeds, confessions, and catechisms of the Presbyterian Church (U.S.A.) offer valuable theological and historical insight on worship in the Reformed tradition; these sources are indicated with numerical citations of the *Book of Confessions* (as in the first paragraph above). I have also included occasional quotations from John Calvin's *Institutes of the Christian Religion*; these are labeled *Institutes*, followed by book, chapter, and section numbers. The Directory for Worship, found in our *Book of Order*, is the constitutional document describing the theology and practice of worship in this denomination; references to the Directory for Worship begin with W, as in W-1.0101. Finally, our *Book of Common Worship* (revised in 2018) provides models for worship, additional texts for various occasions, and theological and pastoral commentary on the liturgy.

To glorify and enjoy God forever. In a sense, that is the answer to every question in this book. I pray that it will inspire, inform, and equip the church and its members in fulfilling that "chief end."

1

Worship Basics

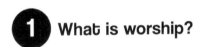 **What is worship?**

The word *worship* comes from an Old English root: "worth-ship."
It suggests something or someone worthy of honor, glory, and
praise. As a noun, *worship* can mean an act of reverence, a religious practice, or a feeling of respect. It is, in ordinary and universal use, a sign of worth.

But for Christians, it might be better to think of worship as a
verb. To worship is to love the one who first loved us. To worship
is to bless the one from whom all blessings flow. To worship is to
show our gratitude for God's amazing grace. To worship is to give
your life to the giver of life.

For Christians, worship is a Trinitarian event. Our worship is
always directed *to God, through Jesus Christ, in the Holy Spirit.*
This is why many of our prayers and hymns end with some version
of this Trinitarian doxology (expression of praise). The holy, triune
God is the only one worthy of our worship. Jesus is our model and
mediator, the one who shows us what true worship is and the one
through whose grace we stand in God's presence. The Holy Spirit
reveals God's gracious word and action and empowers our grateful response.

For Christians, worship and service are two sides of the same
coin. In fact, in biblical Hebrew, "worship" and "serve" are two
meanings of the same word, *'abad* (see Exod. 8:1, e.g.). The word
liturgy comes from the Greek term *leitourgia*, meaning "work of
the people" or "public service" (see Heb. 8:6). There should be no

contradiction between our Sunday worship of God and our daily service of God. Our words and actions in the sanctuary are always connected with what we say and do in the street. As we are called to show our love to God in worship, so we are called to show God's love to our neighbors in the world.

Therefore, to worship means to lead a life worth living—a life that honors the giver of our life and makes a positive difference in the lives of others. In short, it's the only thing worth doing.

2 Why do we worship?

We worship to glorify and enjoy God (see the introduction). The purpose of worship is to give blessing and honor and praise and thanksgiving to God. In good times and in bad, in joy and in sorrow, we glorify the giver of our life. Even—or especially—when we're not enjoying life very much, through the worship of God we experience the deep promise and joy of life restored and made new in Christ. We worship God because God is God. We worship because God *is*.

But let me tell you a secret. There are other good things that happen when we worship God. You might think of them as positive side effects or fringe benefits, overflowing from the gracious abundance of God.

Worship builds relationships and forms community. When we gather in God's presence, we draw closer to one another in the body of Christ. Worship teaches faith and shapes discipleship. When we hear God's word, we learn and grow as believers and followers of Christ. Worship feeds our souls and fills our hearts. When we enjoy Communion with Christ, we are nourished by the grace of God. Worship inspires action and equips for service. When we are sent out in Jesus' name, we go forth to show God's righteousness, justice, and mercy to others.

We have to be very careful that we never mistake these side effects or fringe benefits for the main thing: giving glory to God. When building relationships and forming community become the main thing, worship becomes a social club. When teaching faith and shaping discipleship become the main thing, worship becomes a school. When feeding souls and filling hearts become the main thing, worship becomes a museum or concert. When inspiring action and equipping for service become the main thing, worship becomes a political rally.

So we keep returning to the main thing, the real purpose of worship: to glorify and enjoy the holy, triune God—made known to us in Scripture, made present by the Holy Spirit, and made flesh in Jesus Christ. This is our lighthouse, our landmark. As long as worship is God-directed, God will keep us in faithful paths and pour out the blessings of deep relationships, strong faith, abiding wonder, and inspired service.

3 Do Christians really have to *go* to worship?

Why do we need to attend worship services? Isn't what we believe and how we live more important? In fact, what we believe, how we worship, and how we live are deeply and inextricably connected. Like a three-legged stool, if any of these elements is missing, we lose our balance, and the life of discipleship cannot be supported or sustained.

Early Christians knew this very well. In the fourth century, those who wanted to join the church were expected to memorize the Apostles' Creed (what we believe), the Lord's Prayer (how we pray or worship), and the Ten Commandments (how we live). The sixteenth-century Protestant Reformers also understood this. They wrote catechisms around those same core texts, with questions and answers to elaborate on their implications for Christian faith, Christian worship, and Christian life.

These three aspects of Christian formation may also be connected with the distinguishing marks of the church in the Reformed tradition. John Calvin said that the true church is found where the Word of God (what we believe) is preached and heard and where the sacraments are celebrated (how we worship) according to Christ's institution. The Scots Confession added a third note—ecclesiastical discipline (how we live) uprightly administered.

There remains in the Reformed tradition a strong emphasis on common faith, corporate worship, and public life. In the Presbyterian Church, we seek the mind of Christ (what we believe) together through communal discernment in the councils of the church (as in sessions, presbyteries, and General Assemblies). We experience the saving grace of God (whom we worship) together, especially through the gifts of Word and sacrament. We strive to follow the way of the Spirit (how we live) together in our common life and witness in the world.

These days, it is common to hear people talk about church membership in terms of "believing, belonging, and behaving." This is but a new variation on an old theme. Being a part of the body of Christ is about a common faith (believing), grounded in the Word; a common identity (belonging), forged in worship; and a common way of life (behaving), carried out in the world. Each of these things informs and influences the others as facets of the whole. None of them can stand without the others.

So yes, Christians do need worship. In fact, our faith and life depend on it. To put it another way: through worship we come to have faith in the holy, triune God—on whom our lives depend.

4 What are the essentials of Christian worship?

This is a frequently asked question—and, to be honest, one that I don't find particularly helpful. Too often, this kind of thinking leads to a deadly combination of liturgical minimalism and legalism—a short checklist of nonnegotiables. Pretty soon someone is asking, "What can we get away with omitting?" and "What's the least we have to do to hold a valid service of worship?" And that's not the kind of thinking that glorifies God or edifies God's people.

Our Directory for Worship, part of the Presbyterian Church (U.S.A.) *Book of Order*, offers a better way to approach the matter.

Like a compass, the Directory for Worship orients us to primary things in the theology and practice of worship. (We use it together with a "map," such as the *Book of Common Worship*, in order to navigate the landscape of the liturgy.) The opening chapter of the Directory for Worship provides a helpful overview of these primary things.

First, and fittingly, the Directory for Worship points to the grace and glory of the triune God (W-1.01). It emphasizes God's initiative in worship and describes our participation as a response to God's saving love. It underscores the church's encounter with Jesus Christ in Word and sacrament. It shows how the Holy Spirit uses these gifts to illuminate and serve the nature and purpose of the church.

Second, the Directory for Worship explores the grand and cosmic themes of time, space, and matter (W-1.02) as they relate to Christian worship. We worship in time, devoting hours, days, and seasons to the Lord. We worship in space, setting aside particular places for an encounter with the Holy One. We worship with matter, using the good gifts of creation as signs of God's grace and our gratitude.

Third, the Directory for Worship discusses human language, symbols, and culture (W-1.03). Christian worship relies on ordinary words to convey the wisdom and wonder of the God who is beyond our comprehension. Christian worship uses simple symbols as signs of God's mighty and merciful work of salvation. Christian worship inhabits the challenge and complexity of human culture, just as God came to dwell among us in Jesus Christ.

As the Directory for Worship demonstrates, the real "essentials" of Christian worship are not elements of the liturgy, such as "confession and pardon," "sermon," "great thanksgiving," or "blessing and charge." The real essentials are so much bigger and more important—graceful acts of God and grateful human responses; cosmic gifts of God's creation; living communities of faith and faithfulness. When we focus on these broader horizons, we are less likely to get lost in the weeds of minimalism and legalism. When we are oriented to these primary things, the other elements seem to fall into place.

5 What if there are some parts of worship I hate?

Christian worship was never intended to be a walk in the park, a ride on a roller coaster, or a day at the spa. There are always going to be parts of worship that challenge us, that we find less than thrilling, and that make us uncomfortable. That's the nature of the gospel—the message of Jesus Christ. That's the nature of the lives to which we are called as followers of Jesus. And that's the nature of worship.

But what if there are some parts of worship that deeply trouble you? What if there are elements in worship that make it hard for you to be open to God, true to yourself, and present with others? What should you do? Here are four suggestions, not necessarily in order of importance.

Engage in some honest reflection and self-examination about the source of the problem. Is there something in particular that is bothering you? Is there something that you're resisting? Where do these feelings come from? Ask God for insight and help.

Talk to others about these elements of the service. What do they enjoy or appreciate, and why? What do they struggle with, and why? Let their experience inform and perhaps expand your own.

Study the theology and practice of worship. Learn more about what is happening in the service and why. The Presbyterian Church (U.S.A.) has a great resource called the Directory for Worship that offers clear, accessible descriptions of the patterns and purposes of the liturgy.

Ask questions of pastors, elders, and other worship planners and leaders. They may be grateful for the feedback and able to share some wisdom. They may even agree that there is room for improvement and help to identify a plan for addressing your concern.

Finally, remember that worship is a communal experience: we share in worship with the whole body of Christ. Something that is off-putting to you may be life-giving for others, and vice versa. Remember that worship is a lifelong practice: we experience things differently in different seasons of life. Something that seems to drain you now may sustain you later. Above all, remember that worship isn't about individual preferences or personal satisfaction; it's about loving and serving God and one another in Jesus' name.

2

Leadership and Participation

6 Who directs the worship service?

There are three answers to this question.

First, the theological answer: The one who directs our worship is God. God always makes the first move. In the Reformed/Presbyterian tradition, we understand everything in Christian faith, life, and worship to be a grateful response to God's gracious initiative, particularly through Jesus Christ and in the power of the Holy Spirit. God also has the last word. The source and standard of our worship is the Word of God revealed in Scripture; again, the Word made known to us is none other than Jesus Christ, revealed by the gift of the Holy Spirit. God is the one who calls us to worship, and God is the one who calls us to account for our worship and service in Jesus' name.

Second, the constitutional answer: In terms of the order and organization of the Presbyterian Church, the conduct of worship is subject to the authority of the denomination's Constitution, which is composed of the *Book of Confessions* and the *Book of Order.* Specifically, the Directory for Worship (found in the *Book of Order*) "presents standards and norms for worship" and "shall be authoritative for this church" (preface to the Directory for Worship). At a congregational level, the service of worship is under the direction of the session, a church council composed of ruling elders serving alongside the teaching elder(s) or pastor(s) of the congregation. (For responsibilities of elders and pastors, see W-2.03 in the Directory for Worship.)

Third, the liturgical answer: In a service of worship, there is generally a "presider" (usually the pastor), who—ideally after a great deal of consultation and collaboration with others—helps worshipers find their way through the liturgy. This person is not like a schoolmaster, a factory floor manager, or an orchestra conductor. It might be better to think of the presider as a skillful tour guide or shepherd. With patience, grace, and loving care, the presider leads the people to green pastures and still waters, through deep valleys to the table that God prepares. In short, a good presider simply follows the Good Shepherd.

And here is where the three answers converge. The goal of the liturgy is theological: to point to what God is doing in worship and in the world. The objective of the Constitution is also theological: to assure that the church's worship and service remain faithful to the Word and Spirit of God, who alone directs our worship and to whom our worship is directed.

 ## What does it mean to participate in worship?

If worship really has something to do with the meaning of life—to glorify and enjoy God now and always (see the introduction)—then participating in worship must be kind of a big deal. When it comes to the meaning and purpose of life, we don't want to be passive bystanders.

Fortunately, Jesus had something to say about the meaning and purpose of human life. A lawyer asked Jesus which commandment was the greatest (see Matt. 22 and Mark 12); in another version of the story, the question is about what one must do to inherit eternal life (see Luke 10). It was a trick question, but naturally Jesus aced the exam. First he quoted Deuteronomy: "You shall love the LORD your God with all your heart, and with all your soul, and with all your might" (Deut. 6:5); then Leviticus: "You shall love your neighbor as yourself" (Lev. 19:18).

The Gospels of Matthew, Mark, and Luke break it down in various ways—heart, soul, mind, strength—as the Hebrew and

Hellenistic (Greek) cultures had different ideas about the seat of human emotions, intellect, and will. But it doesn't really matter how you parse it. The point is clear: Give everything—all that you are, all that you have—give it all to God in love and service. And a second commandment is like it: Just as God has loved us—fully, holding nothing back, and to the end—in this way, let us love one another (see John 13 and 1 John 4).

This is, in fact, what participating in worship is all about: loving God and neighbor with heart, mind, soul, and strength. There is a vertical (divine/human) dimension: we lift our hearts to God, offering up the joys and struggles of human life; we open our minds to God, seeking holy wisdom and asking honest questions; we bare our souls before God, entrusting our secret hopes and fears, pride and shame; and we use our strength for God, giving our time, talent, and treasure to serve God's will in the world. There is a horizontal (human/human) dimension, too: we seek to love others—within and beyond the sanctuary—with all the gifts and capacities God has given us: heart, mind, soul, and strength.

Little wonder, then, that the revolutionary reforms to the Roman Catholic liturgy launched in the 1960s at the Second Vatican Council called for "full, active, and conscious participation" in worship. Another way to say it might be with all your heart, soul, strength, and mind. We Presbyterians have our own beloved phrase for this concept, found in questions asked when deacons, elders, and ministers are ordained: Will you serve with "energy, intelligence, imagination, and love" (*Book of Order*, W-4.0404h)? However you say it, the worship of the eternal, living God deserves and demands our all.

8 Doesn't participation involve a speaking part?

Not necessarily. Maybe it started in the fifteenth century with the printing press. For all the benefits of the new accessibility of the written word, one of the downsides is that we have grown accustomed to worshiping God with our noses buried in a book or bulletin. Affordable photocopiers definitely exacerbated the situation. Extraterrestrial anthropologists might well assume that the worship of our God involves the sacrifice of many trees.

Maybe it started in the eighteenth century with Sunday schools. For all the blessings of this important movement in Christian education, one of the negative results was the proliferation of long, printed unison prayers and responsive litanies that had more to do with the instruction of the congregation than the worship of God.

However it happened, liturgy came to be equated with literacy. We have come to assume that active participation in worship has something to do with the bold print in the bulletin. When I'm speaking, I'm participating; when the leader is speaking, I'm not. I refer to this as the traffic-signal theory of participation.

Ideally, however, we are all participating *throughout* the service of worship. The most basic form of participation is simply showing up: by your presence, you help to assemble the body of Christ for worship. I'd argue that the most important form of participation, however, is prayer: opening oneself to the presence of God. Prayer can involve words directed to God, aloud or in silence. But prayer can take many other forms: listening, looking, walking, dancing, breathing, centering, singing, silence. Prayer can happen in the form of certain postures or gestures, with or without words: standing, kneeling, or bowing; lifting, clasping, or stretching out one's hands. The important thing is simply to focus on God, through Jesus Christ, in the Holy Spirit.

Of course, our focus will wax and wane; our thoughts will drift; our minds will wander. It is also true that particular words, songs, and actions can become so familiar that we may forget they are meant to be prayer. When these things happen, remember that it is just another opportunity to practice what Christian life is all about—another chance to turn to God, to say, "Amen" and "Here I am," to make our grateful response to God's gracious action.

9 Why do certain people have special roles?

It all goes back to baptism in the name of the Trinity. In his first letter to the church at Corinth, the apostle Paul wrote, "Now there are varieties of gifts, but the same Spirit; and there are varieties of services, but the same Lord; and there are varieties of activities, but it is the same God who activates all of them in everyone" (1 Cor. 12:4–6). Notice the Trinitarian pattern of this teaching on spiritual gifts: a threefold statement naming Spirit, Lord, and God. The diversity of spiritual gifts in the body of Christ is linked with our baptism in the name of the triune God.

Paul makes this clear: "For just as the body is one and has many members, and all the members of the body, though many, are one body, so it is with Christ. For in the one Spirit we were all baptized into the one body" (1 Cor. 12:12–13). The very nature of the triune God involves unity and diversity—One-in-Three and Three-in-One. Similarly, in Christ's church the many are united for the common good.

So the Holy Spirit bestows many, different gifts upon the body of Christ, all for the service of God and God's people. When we come to worship, we seek to use these gifts together for God's glory. Because the Spirit pours out these gifts so freely, anyone may be invited to lead prayer, read Scripture, or contribute to worship in a variety of other ways if they have been properly prepared and equipped to do so.

In the Presbyterian/Reformed tradition, three special roles should be mentioned: deacons, ruling elders, and ministers of Word and Sacrament. These are the three "orders of ministry" to which members may be ordained when the church discerns that God has called and equipped them for particular forms of service.

Deacons are called to the ministries of compassion, witness, and service. For this reason, it is especially appropriate for deacons to offer prayers of intercession, read Scripture, and lead the charge to serve God in the world.

Ruling elders are called to the ministries of nurture, discernment, and governance. For this reason, they have oversight over the congregation's worship; it is also especially appropriate for ruling elders to lead prayer, read Scripture, serve Communion, and occasionally teach the Word.

And ministers of Word and Sacrament are—you guessed it—called to the ministry of Word and Sacrament. This means that pastors are ordinarily the ones to preach the sermon and lead in the celebration of the sacraments. However, there are a few other actions in worship—connected with the gifts of Word and sacrament—that are especially appropriate for the pastor's leadership. These include the declaration of forgiveness (sometimes spoken at the baptismal font) and the blessing at the conclusion of the service—both "echoes" of the same good news proclaimed in the sermon.

10 What kind of worship will attract young people?

This common question betrays a lack of respect for young people, a lack of understanding about worship, and a lack of trust in God.

Let's start with God. God is the one who chooses us as beloved children, even before our birth. And God is the one who calls us to worship. This means when young people come to worship, it's because God calls and sends them. Our primary calling is to welcome those whom God sends into our midst, discern their gifts for ministry in Jesus' name, and share in their formation for Christian worship and service.

Now, about worship. Worship isn't a technology or set of techniques we use to accomplish our goals. It's a transforming encounter with God. To be sure, countless blessings will flow from this encounter, but the point of worship is to worship. Whenever we start trying to engineer worship to accomplish secondary goals, we're asking for trouble (see question 2).

As for young people, they turn out to be as wonderfully multifaceted and unpredictable as any other demographic group. They generally enjoy thinking for themselves, react negatively to condescension, and are savvy enough to know when they're being hustled.

We *have* learned a few things from generational studies in recent decades, and it's tempting to try to apply those insights to worship. While there is surely some truth to the idea of a generational "spirit of the times"—common concerns, distinctive characteristics, pivotal events—the problem is that these qualities are much easier to understand in hindsight. By the time we can identify them, they're already passing us by as a new generation arrives on the scene.

Over all these objections, I suppose if forced to answer the original question—What kind of worship will attract more young people?—I would have to say the same kind of worship that anyone would find compelling: (1) faithful, vibrant worship in Word and sacrament, (2) rooted in an authentic, welcoming community that (3) extends itself in service to God in the world.

11 What should we do with children in worship?

We should worship with them!

In recent decades, too many congregations have gotten into the habit of holding Sunday school at the same time as worship or dismissing children and youth to other special programing while adults attend the regular service. Then they are surprised and disappointed when those same children and youth grow up and decide not to participate in worship. But how can we expect children to enjoy and appreciate something they've never had the chance to experience in their formative years? Why would they suddenly want to take part in an event where they've always been made to feel unwelcome?

Some congregations hold special worship services for children at the same time as the adult service, with the idea that these separate opportunities will teach children how to worship. The problem is that this deprives everyone of the fullness of what Christian worship can be. Children, youth, and adults bring different gifts to worship, and they need one another in order to be the whole body of Christ. Adults benefit from the energy and imagination of children and from the passions and questions of youth. Youth and children benefit from the wisdom and patience of adults.

Besides, the most effective way for children and youth to learn how to worship is by simply worshiping with the whole congregation. In language acquisition it is called the "total immersion" method; learning to worship is no different. When children and youth are immersed in the community of the baptized, they quickly absorb the prayers, songs, patterns, and practices of Christian worship and have a better chance of retaining them. As with learning a new language, it's critical that children have this formative experience on a regular basis and at an early age.

As for engaging children and youth in the service, children's bulletins or other kid- and youth-friendly guides to worship can make the liturgy more accessible. Children's bags with art supplies—ideally marked or decorated with the children's names— can help to engage the active minds and hands of the youngest worshipers. Other adults are often eager to sit with children as worship mentors or "substitute grandparents" so that parents can focus on preaching and prayer. It is helpful for each sermon to include at least one section or illustration that will connect with younger listeners; indeed, when this happens there may not be the need for a separate children's sermon. Shorter prayers, especially when interspersed with repeated refrains or gestures, also help children to stay tuned in to the liturgy. In general, a more embodied approach to worship leadership and participation will stand a better chance of connecting with younger worshipers. Congregations sometimes set aside a special area for children in the back of the sanctuary or in a side room, but children will be more engaged and involved in worship if they have preferred seating near the front—where the action is.

Yes, worshiping with children will bring challenges to the community of faith. Worship might be a little louder, messier, more chaotic. Adults may find themselves a little more distracted, at least at first. But the blessings of worshiping together as the whole people of God far outweigh these inconveniences.

12 How can we make worship more seeker-friendly?

The most powerful, effective way of drawing others into Christian life is to live that life as fully as you can, as an offering of thanks and praise for the grace of God. Here are seven ideas on how to do that. These are not intended to be a road map for renewal or strategies for success; in fact, they may be counterintuitive, contradicting conventional wisdom on church growth.

Embrace mystery. Seekers are seeking something . . . and it's probably not a lecture on Presbyterian worship. Let songs, symbols, and silence speak. Don't try fill up every space in the service with explanations for things we scarcely understand. Just point to the glory of God.

Keep it simple. The beauty of Christian worship is that it doesn't require many ingredients—word, water, bread, and cup; the gathering of the beloved body of Christ; the sending of God's people in mission to the world. Focus on those things—as though your life depends on them. They are signs of the saving grace of God.

Be who you are. Inauthenticity stinks, and seekers can smell it a mile away. Be the "aroma of Christ" (2 Cor. 2:15). Bear witness to what Christ is doing among you, in your own awesomely awkward, clumsily charming way. Don't try to be who you think seekers want you to be. But . . .

Be ready to change. Newcomers will bring new songs, new prayers, new offerings, and yes, new challenges. They'll change the way you worship. Receive this as a gift, with gratitude. Christian life is a pilgrimage. Seekers may be God's way of saying, "Keep moving."

Love your neighbors. Get to know your neighborhood. Contribute to your community. And when you gather for worship, *pray* for that community; collect items for the food bank; recruit volunteers for the soup kitchen and community garden. Get involved.

Love one another. This is how people will know you are Jesus' disciples (John 13:35): how you shake hands before the service begins, how you embrace at the passing of the peace, how you lift

one another up in prayer, how you stoop down to serve Communion to children, and so on.

Love God . . . and just worship. Worship God with joy, with
delight, with abandon. Let go of your anxiety about "doing it
right." Only God is holy. Nothing will be more compelling or
attractive to the seekers in your midst than authentic prayer and
praise to the true and living God.

13 Why do we use songs and prayers from other cultures?

When we gather for worship we are surrounded by a "great cloud
of witnesses" (Heb. 12:1)—not only in the place we are worshiping but across the global, ecumenical church and throughout history. Songs and prayers from other cultures help us to remember
that Christian worship is an ancient, worldwide phenomenon and
that our expression of the faith is just one small part of that great
diversity of Christ's body—the communion of saints in every time
and place.

This is how the Christian church began. The Holy Spirit
descended on the disciples at Pentecost, giving them the ability
to speak in other languages, proclaiming the mighty acts of God
(Acts 2:4, 11). As Peter explained, this was the promise of the
prophet Joel: that the Spirit of God would be poured out on all flesh
so that everyone who calls on the name of the Lord would be saved
(Acts 2:21; cf. Joel 2:32).

Elements of worship from other times and places also keep us
mindful that in Jesus Christ God's Word became flesh in a setting
very different from our own. This is sometimes called the "scandal
of the incarnation"—that God would dwell among us as a particular person, in a particular place, in a particular time. But this same
scandal amounts to the good news of the gospel—that God would
seek us out, in our place, and in our time, to claim us as beloved
children and offer us the gift of eternal, abundant life in Christ.

Furthermore, learning unfamiliar songs and prayers helps us
to remember that the gospel of Jesus Christ *is* strange—even

countercultural. Jesus calls us to a new and different way of life that challenges the patterns and practices of the world around us. We are invited to become citizens of God's realm, a new heaven and earth, where justice, righteousness, and peace will reign.

Songs and prayers from other cultures also enable us to pray in solidarity with others around the world, with people in very different situations. When we hear of a conflict or crisis in a particular place, a hymn or prayer that comes from that part of the world can help to strengthen the ties that bind us together as a human family. Having sung and prayed together in this way, we may be more likely to speak up for justice and reach out in compassion.

Finally, the vision of Revelation suggests that this kind of worship is precisely what's in store for us in the realm of heaven:

> After this I looked, and there was a great multitude that no one could count, from every nation, from all tribes and peoples and languages, standing before the throne and before the Lamb, robed in white, with palm branches in their hands. They cried out in a loud voice, saying,
>
> > "Salvation belongs to our God
> > who is seated on the
> > throne, and to the Lamb!"
> > (Rev. 7:9–10)

Indeed, we are surrounded by a great cloud of witnesses, in this life and in the life to come.

3

The Order of Worship

14 What is the order of worship?

The best place to start in understanding the order of worship is a
little village about seven miles from Jerusalem: Emmaus.

According to Luke it was the first day of the week, the same
day Jesus rose from the dead. Two disciples are walking along the
road and are joined by a mysterious stranger. They pour out their
hearts to him, confessing their doubts and fears. Then the stranger
begins to interpret the Scriptures to them, showing how the sacred
texts point to the coming of the Messiah. They stop for the night
and ask the stranger to stay with them. When he is at table with
them, he takes bread, blesses and breaks it, and gives it to them.
Suddenly their eyes are opened, and they recognize Jesus, but he
vanishes from their sight. Now their hearts are burning with the
joy of the risen Lord. The disciples get up that very hour to return
to Jerusalem to tell their companions the good news: The Lord has
risen indeed!

There it is—our pattern of worship for the Lord's Day, the day
of resurrection. At the center is Word and Table: interpreting the
Scriptures in light of the risen Lord, and sharing the meal that
Christ prepares for us. These central actions are framed by gathering and sending: meeting in the presence of Christ and going forth
in the power of the Spirit. Christians have been doing this for two
thousand years, beginning with Emmaus.

Aspects of the order of worship can be traced to a variety of
other sources—Jewish synagogue services and temple practices,

traditions of the first Christian communities, developments from the early church through the Middle Ages, contributions of the Protestant Reformers, along with the social histories and cultural contexts of Christians around the world. But the heart of the order of worship for the Lord's Day is what those disciples experienced on the road to Emmaus: meeting Jesus in Word and sacrament.

Significantly, these essential elements correspond with John Calvin's notes of the true church: "Wherever we see the Word of God purely preached and heard, and the sacraments administered according to Christ's institution, there, it is not to be doubted, a church of God exists" (*Institutes* 4.1.9). It is no coincidence that these distinguishing marks of Christian worship are also the vital signs of Christ's church.

Of course, the Gospels tell many other stories of Jesus' gathering disciples, teaching God's way, breaking bread, and sending apostles. This pattern of action in Jesus' life and ministry continues through the worship and service of all who claim him as Savior and Lord.

15 Why does the order of worship matter?

The word *order* carries a lot of baggage—especially when it travels among Presbyterians. The notion that "all things should be done decently and in order" (1 Cor. 14:40) is an unofficial motto for us. Indeed, we are experts at ordering an agenda for a meeting. Yet, as "Protestants," we also have a long tradition of questioning authority, and we don't like to take orders from anyone—other than God.

This seems to be especially true when it comes to the order of worship. The "regulative principle" of worship, held among many churches of the Reformed tradition, is the idea that our liturgical practices must conform to the teachings of the Bible—limiting our patterns of worship to those commended in the Scriptures and rejecting those that the Scriptures forbid. One of our sixteenth-century confessions even provides a long Greek word to describe the danger of "self-devised worship"—*ethelothreskia* (Col. 2:23; see *Book of Confessions*, 5.116).

Given these historical dynamics, Presbyterian worship has come to be marked by a dynamic relationship between an order or form of worship and the freedom to be spontaneous. Our Directory for Worship explains it well: "Fixed forms of worship are valuable in that they offer consistent patterns and practices that help to shape lives of faith and faithfulness. More spontaneous approaches to worship are valuable in that they provide space for unexpected insight and inspiration. In whatever form it takes, worship is to be ordered by God's Word and open to the creativity of the Holy Spirit" (*Book of Order*, W-2.0102).

The "order" of worship is not intended to be a set of rules; neither should it be experienced as an agenda or checklist. Consider a more organic metaphor—a tree. The order of worship keeps us rooted and grounded in faith yet remains flexible enough to weather the winds of change. It helps us live together in the love of God, grow together in the grace of Christ, and bear good fruit together in the community of the Spirit. Or consider the classic biblical image of the body. Every part is different but connected. Heart, mind, soul, and strength work together for the good of the whole. The health of the body depends on regular exercise (participation in worship) and a balanced diet (Word and sacrament).

To put it another way, the order of worship is a set of patterns and practices that nurture and nourish us as God's people. We are people who gather together in the name of the triune God, listen together to the story of God's saving love, eat together at the table Christ prepares, and go forth together in the power of the Spirit to serve God in the world. As we do these things—week by week, slowly but surely—through the shape of worship God shapes us.

16 Why do Presbyterians say confession every week?

The short answer: because we all fall hopelessly short of the glory of God. We constantly fail in our love for God and for our neighbors. We desperately need God's grace. We are sinners. But we are baptized sinners, thanks be to God. This is how we know God's grace is with us. This is why we never give up in trying to love God and neighbor. This is how we can see glimpses of God's glory, even in this world so stained by sin.

As Paul wrote to the church in Rome, "Do you not know that all of us who have been baptized into Christ Jesus were baptized into his death?" (Rom. 6:3). The apostle goes on to explain that through our crucifixion with Christ, the body of sin is destroyed; because we have been raised to new life with Christ, we are no longer captives or slaves to sin. Therefore, Paul concludes, "you also must consider yourself dead to sin and alive to God in Christ Jesus" (Rom. 6:11).

For this reason, it is a source of great grace and peace for us to join with the rest of the baptized in confessing our sin. It isn't a weekly guilt trip. First, it is an honest and natural response to the holiness of God that we encounter when we gather for worship: God is holy; we are not (see Isaiah 6). Second, it is an important part of our preparation to hear the Word and celebrate the sacraments. And third, it is a regular rehearsal of the work of reconciliation God calls us to do throughout our lives.

Typically, in Reformed worship the time of confession and pardon begins with an unequivocal assurance of God's love and mercy. Because we trust the grace of God, we can open our hearts before God with confidence, knowing that God is ready to forgive us. So that is what we do. In silence and spoken prayer we confess our own sins and lament the evil around us. We boldly ask for God's grace so that we might lead new lives in the light of Christ's resurrection. And then the minister gives voice to the good news of this divine mercy: "I declare to you in the name of Jesus Christ, we are forgiven."

Leading the confession and pardon at the baptismal font emphasizes the connection between the gift of baptism and God's redeeming love. Pouring water suggests the grace of God that overflows for us despite our sin. Praying around the font helps to convey the depth of God's great mercy, deeper than our transgressions. Lifting water evokes the freedom and joy of new life in the risen Lord.

One of the strengths of our Presbyterian/Reformed tradition is that we take sin so seriously as to say the confession every week. As those who have been crucified with Christ, we can no longer live in denial of the evil in the world or the sin in our own hearts. But as those who are risen to new life with Christ, we are even more serious about God's amazing grace.

17 Why is there an offering during worship?

The offering is a sign of our grateful response to God's gracious action in Jesus Christ. This rhythm of grace and gratitude is a pervasive pattern in Christian faith, life, and worship in the Reformed tradition, shaping who we are and how we are called to live. So while it generally includes the collection of financial gifts, the offering in Christian worship is about much more than this. It is about giving our lives to the giver of life. It is about loving the one who first loved us—heart, mind, soul, and strength—and loving our neighbors as ourselves, following Jesus' example.

In the Service for the Lord's Day, with its pattern of Word and sacrament, the offering is the first movement of the liturgy for the Lord's Supper, part of our turning to the table. As Jesus took bread—a sign of his body, broken and given for us, we offer ourselves to God, a sacrifice of thanks and praise. The word *Eucharist*, meaning thanksgiving, conveys this central theme of gratitude for God's grace. Even when Communion is not included, the offering points to the Table and provides a way for us to make our grateful response to the Word proclaimed. It is a sign of our great thanksgiving for God's grace, an expression of our love for God and neighbor, and a chance to foster the practice of gratitude in daily life.

In recent years, people are asking what we should do with the offering now that many people are making financial contributions online. A variety of imaginative possibilities emerge. The offering could be a time to make a special contribution to a critical need in the church or world—above and beyond members' regular financial commitments. It could be a time to invite support for a community service project, neighborhood outreach, or movement for social change. It could be a time to lift up creative gifts within the congregation—whether a choral anthem, children's artwork, or handcrafted goods.

When the Eucharist is celebrated, the offering provides a time to prepare the table by bringing forth the bread and cup(s) for the sacrament in joyful procession. Regardless of whether the Lord's Supper is celebrated on a given week, this can be a time to gather canned goods or other nonperishables for the church food pantry or a local soup kitchen. Children may be invited to help collect these items and place them at the foot of the Communion table.

18 Is it charge and blessing or blessing and charge?

Recent Presbyterian Church (U.S.A.) worship resources—including the 2013 hymnal *Glory to God*, the 2017 revision to the Directory for Worship, and the 2018 *Book of Common Worship*—have suggested that the blessing (or benediction) be followed by the charge at the conclusion of the Service for the Lord's Day. This order represents a reversal of the charge-and-blessing pattern in the 1993 *Book of Common Worship*. What's behind this change?

First, there is a theological reason. God tells Abraham and Sarah, "'I will bless you . . . so that you will be a blessing'" (Gen. 12:2). We are blessed (benediction) in order to be a blessing (charge) to others. God blesses us, then we go out to share God's blessing with our neighbors. This reflects the Reformed understanding of God's initiative in all things: God acts (benediction), we respond (charge). It is also connected with the great Reformed theme of grace and gratitude: God is gracious to us (benediction), and we show our gratitude by how we live (charge).

Second, there is an ecclesiological reason—one related to the nature and purpose of the church. Current scholars and leaders have highlighted the "missional" nature of the church, demonstrating that our very reason for being in the body of Christ is to share the life of Christ with the world. The order of blessing and charge is like an arrow, pointing from the church Christ has called to the world God loves and leading us out to share in the Spirit's work.

Third, there is a liturgical reason. Ending worship with the charge puts a stronger accent on "sending," the final element of the Service for the Lord's Day. It underscores the "work of the people" in the world, our call to worship God through the service of daily living. When the blessing follows the charge, there is a greater potential for stalling the missional momentum of the service.

Fourth, there is a pastoral reason—one related to collegiality and mutuality in ministry. While the church's pastor is ordinarily the one who speaks the blessing, the charge may be spoken by a ruling elder, deacon, or other leader in the congregation (even a child who is assisting with worship leadership for the day). The order of blessing and charge thus gives someone other than the pastor the last word, lifting up the roles of other spiritual leaders in the congregation in contributing to the church's mission.

Finally, there is an ecumenical reason. The pattern of blessing and charge is a more familiar one in many other Christian traditions. As worshipers move from church to church, as congregations explore ecumenical collaboration, and as pastors are granted permission to minister in other denominations, it is helpful to have a common order of worship.

There are times, such as pastoral services, when the order of charge followed by blessing may be more appropriate or when the blessing may stand alone. The funeral is a good example. On these occasions, we especially need to remember that God has the last word, and that word is a blessing.

19 Should Presbyterian worship be traditional, contemporary, or blended?

All of the above!

Presbyterian worship is traditional in that it is grounded in Scripture, established on the practices of the ancient and ecumenical church, and guided by the principles of our theological ancestors in the Reformation. Faithful worship must also be contemporary: attentive to the present concerns of the church, community, and world; voiced in the common language(s) of the people; and responsive to the leading of God's Word and Spirit in this age. Our worship is always blended; in the profound unity and rich diversity of the body of Christ, with myriad languages, customs, and styles, we join our voices with the saints of every time and place to praise and glorify God.

From this starting point, a more meaningful set of questions emerges: Which traditions and to what ends? Is a particular habit or practice rooted in the heart of Christian tradition or steeped in sentimentality? Does it lead us to fresh revelation or deadening repetition? How can we renew an ancient and valuable pattern of worship? Do some of our traditions exclude the outsider, oppress the powerless, and obscure the faith?

How do we engage our contemporary culture(s) in ways that are faithful and responsive to the gospel? Are the trends of contemporary culture consonant with Christ's realm? What are we communicating about the church, and what is being lost in translation? When are we following the Spirit, and when are we chasing after worldly success?

What blending of ancient and modern is most appropriate for a worshiping community? How do we evoke the fullness of Christian tradition and meaning in different cultural contexts? In a particular worshiping community, whose voices are lifted up most often, and whose are often silenced?

Responding to these deeper and more difficult questions is an integral part of the "work of the people" in Christian liturgy. It requires dialogue, discipline, discernment, and, above all, prayer. In the frequent refrain of the book of Revelation, those who plan and lead Christian worship must continue to "listen to what the Spirit is saying to the churches" (Rev. 2:7, 11, etc.) today.

4

The Word

20 Is there an official version of Scripture?

While some Christian churches have authorized translations of the Scriptures, there is no official version of the Bible for the Presbyterian Church (U.S.A.). Commonly used translations include the New Revised Standard Version (NRSV), the New International Version (NIV), and the Common English Bible (CEB). But none of these is required or even recommended in the denomination's Directory for Worship.

What the Directory for Worship does say is that the church's session—made up of ruling elders and the pastor(s)—is responsible for the selection of Bibles for use by the congregation in worship, along with other books of prayer or song (*Book of Order*, W-2.0305). The minister of Word and Sacrament is responsible for selecting the version of the Scriptures that is to be read aloud in public worship (W-3.0301). This translation should reflect the common language(s) of the congregation, and the minister should let worshipers know if the biblical text comes from an unusual translation or has been significantly adapted.

While there is no official version of Scripture, it should be noted that the Reformed tradition puts a high value on faithfulness to the original languages of the biblical text. Seminarians are expected to study Hebrew and Greek so that they will be better able to understand, appreciate, and interpret the nuances of the Scriptures. Another strong value in the Presbyterian Church (U.S.A.) is ecumenical partnership. An ecumenically developed translation of

Scripture tends to be more sensitive to diverse Christian perspectives and experiences and helps to keep us "on the same page" with other members of the body of Christ. Accordingly, we generally favor versions of the Bible that reflect careful, scholarly work with the biblical languages and extensive consultation with representatives from other denominations.

While a loose paraphrase or personal interpretation of the Scripture may be helpful as a sermon illustration or a teaching device, worshipers need to be able to trust that the words presented as God's word come from "the church's book." Then, when the reader says, "The word of the Lord," the people will be able to respond with confidence, "Thanks be to God."

21 What is the lectionary, and where does it come from?

A lectionary is a list of Scripture readings designated for use in worship. In some traditions, the word *lectionary* may also refer to a book or set of books containing the full texts of those designated readings. Lectionaries are, by their very nature, selective. They seek to draw out primary stories and themes from the whole witness of Scripture, or to identify relevant passages for a particular event or occasion. Lectionaries may be organized around the Sundays, seasons, and festivals of the Christian year, or they may be designed for reading in daily prayer. Some lectionaries represent centuries of Christian wisdom, following long-standing patterns of readings for particular days or seasons; others, more recently developed, reflect an effort to incorporate different experiences or address gaps in the church's proclamation of the story of salvation.

The most commonly used lectionary in the Presbyterian Church (U.S.A.) is the Revised Common Lectionary (RCL). This lectionary traces its origin to the revisions to the Roman Catholic Lectionary for Mass that emerged out of the Second Vatican Council (1962–1965). With its three-year cycle of readings (A, B, and C), this new Catholic lectionary quickly inspired Protestant adaptations. One of the first such appeared in the 1970 Presbyterian *Worshipbook*. Around this same time, the ecumenical Consultation on Common Texts was established to coordinate lectionary work (preventing the proliferation of many different adaptations) and to promote the use of other common texts in worship. The Consultation first released the 1983 Common Lectionary. After a nine-year period of trial use, the Revised Common Lectionary followed in 1992. This lectionary is now used by various denominations around the world; its roots in the Roman Catholic lectionary keep us connected throughout the ecumenical church.

Other lectionary systems that have been developed in subsequent years include the African American Lectionary (2007), the Narrative Lectionary (2010), and the Year D Project (2012). Preachers and worship planners may also choose to read through particular books of the Bible or organize worship around a series of topical sermons—nevertheless, such sermons should always be based on Scripture.

22 How many readings are required?

There is no hard-and-fast requirement for the number of Scripture passages read in Presbyterian worship. The Directory for Worship says, "Selected readings are to be drawn from both Old and New Testaments, and over a period of time should reflect the broad content and full message of Scripture" (*Book of Order*, W-3.0301). Since the minister of Word and Sacrament is responsible for selecting the Scriptures that will be read on any given Sunday (see W-2.0304), this means the pastor bears the primary responsibility for assuring that worshipers enjoy a well-balanced diet from the feast of God's Word.

The use of a lectionary can help to relieve preachers of this burden. As the Directory for Worship notes, "Lectionaries ensure a broad range of biblical texts as well as consistency and connection with the universal Church" (W-3.0301). In other words, lectionaries tend to offer a more diverse and disciplined pattern of reading than we might design on our own if left to our own devices. They can challenge us to move beyond our favorite books of the Bible and explore texts we wouldn't otherwise consider.

The Revised Common Lectionary provides three readings and a psalm for each Sunday and festival in the Christian year. The first reading is ordinarily drawn from the Old Testament or Hebrew Scriptures; during the season of Easter the first reading comes from the book of Acts. The psalm is a prayerful response to the first reading, ideally engaging the congregation in song. The second reading comes from a New Testament epistle or the book of Revelation. The final reading is always from one of the four Gospels: Matthew, Mark, Luke, and John.

The Directory for Worship also notes that "selections for readings should be guided by the rhythms of the Christian year, events in the world, and pastoral concerns in the local congregation" (W-3.0301). Such times of crisis or celebration may inspire the choice of other readings. Though this is the prerogative of the preacher, it is best to consult with church musicians and worship committees so that the service will remain collaborative in its design and coherent in its organization. As the session is charged to "make provision for the regular preaching of the Word" (W-2.0303), the congregation's ruling elders also have a significant role in nurturing the congregation's regular engagement with the Scriptures.

Beyond the selected readings for the day, other elements of worship can and should be steeped in Scripture—from the opening sentences to the blessing and charge. Regardless of the number of readings chosen, this kind of deep immersion in the language of Scripture will increase our fluency in the faith.

23 Does the sermon have to be so long?

Justin Martyr, writing in the second century, offered this description of early Christian worship: "And on the day called Sunday, all who live in cities or in the country gather together to one place, and the memoirs of the apostles or the writings of the prophets are read, as long as time permits; then, when the reading has ceased, the president verbally instructs, and exhorts to the imitation of these good things" (*First Apology*, 67).

One wonders what Justin meant by "as long as time permits." In any case, it seems clear that early Christians took seriously the proclamation of the Word—just as Presbyterian churches do today. In contemporary preaching, the length of the sermon depends a great deal on liturgical tradition and cultural context. In some communities of faith, worshipers will start checking their watches after ten or fifteen minutes of preaching. In others, the congregation may feel cheated if the sermon clocks in at less than thirty or forty-five minutes.

Of course, the quality of the preaching makes a big difference as well. A ten-minute sermon can feel interminable when it is clear at the outset that the preacher has nothing to say. A skillful preacher can hold forth for half an hour and still leave the congregation wanting more.

This having been said, a strong sermon does not have to be a long one. The truth is that many sermons are longer than they need to be. This tends to happen when preachers lose sight of their primary role, striving instead to be motivational speakers, seminary professors, or stand-up comedians.

While the sermon may well inspire, enlighten, or even entertain, the purpose of Christian preaching is to point to Jesus Christ, crucified and risen. It is to help the church listen to the voice of God, know the Word made flesh, and follow the Spirit of truth. It is to offer the grace and challenge of the gospel to the people of God. When the preacher has this task clearly in mind, good things can come in small packages.

24 Are there other ways to proclaim the gospel?

"Preach the gospel at all times; if necessary, use words." This popular quotation is attributed to Francis of Assisi (c. 1182–1226), an Italian friar and itinerant preacher. Unfortunately, there's no evidence that Francis actually wrote or spoke these words.

The proclamation of the gospel in Christian worship, in fact, depends on words. Proclamation always begins with Scripture, God's word to us in the Old and New Testaments. Proclamation seeks to reveal Jesus Christ, God's Word made flesh. And proclamation involves language, as the preacher attempts to translate the message of the gospel in a particular time and place.

On occasion, the gospel may be proclaimed in ways other than a sermon—drama, music, dance, and visual arts. But in order to serve as Christian proclamation, these forms of creative expression must always be grounded in the Scriptures and seek to illuminate the presence of God's living Word—Jesus Christ.

In some services of worship, the reading of long or multiple passages of Scripture, woven together with song, silence, and prayer, functions as the proclamation of the Word. Examples include the Christmas Lessons and Carols service or the Palm/Passion and Good Friday services of Holy Week. In such services, a time of silence or brief meditation may be sufficient.

The preaching of the Word can, on occasion, take forms other than a traditional sermon—storytelling, poetry, dialogue, conversation, or testimony, to name a few. But these forms of proclamation do not typically take the place of preaching on a regular basis.

The sacraments are also a form of proclamation. John Calvin said, "Let it be regarded as a settled principle that the sacraments have the same office as the word of God: to offer and set forth Christ to us, and in him the treasures of heavenly grace" (*Institutes* 4.14.17). It should be noted, however, that in the Reformed tradition the celebration of the sacraments is always accompanied by the proclamation of the Word, as Word and sacrament together reveal the presence of Jesus Christ.

Finally, the proclamation of the gospel is not the work of the preacher alone. It is the calling of every believer to proclaim the gospel in our daily lives, through word and deed. Christian worship prepares and equips us to bear witness to the good news of Jesus Christ wherever we go.

"Preach the gospel at all times; if necessary, use words." Maybe Francis never uttered or penned those famous words, but maybe he didn't have to. Maybe the message was evident in the way he lived his life.

5

The Sacraments

25 Why do Presbyterians have only two sacraments?

The classic Reformed/Presbyterian answer boils down to this: because Jesus said so. As our Directory for Worship puts it, "The Reformed tradition recognizes the Sacraments of Baptism and the Lord's Supper (also called Eucharist or Holy Communion) as having been instituted by the Lord Jesus Christ through the witness of the Scriptures and sustained through the history of the universal Church" (*Book of Order*, W-3.0401).

The Gospels begin with the call of John to "repent and be baptized," for the realm of God is near; this leads directly to the account of Jesus' own baptism by John in the Jordan River. As with our own baptism, it is depicted as a Trinitarian event—the Holy Spirit descends from the heavens; the voice of God says, "You are my beloved child"; and Christ is at the center of it all. At the conclusion of Matthew's Gospel, Jesus institutes the sacrament of baptism through his Great Commission: "'Go therefore and make disciples of all nations, baptizing them in the name of the Father and of the Son and of the Holy Spirit'" (Matt. 28:19). The theology and practice of baptism is also deeply connected with stories and themes of the Hebrew Scriptures (the creation, the flood, the exodus, e.g.) and developed in other writings of the New Testament (especially Acts and the letters of Paul).

The Gospels are similarly full of stories of Jesus sharing meals with his followers, from the feeding of the multitudes to breaking bread with the disciples after he rose from the dead. All of these meals reveal a similar pattern of action—taking bread, blessing, breaking, and sharing it—a pattern that continues to shape our celebration of the sacrament. When it comes to the institution of the sacrament, we point to a particular meal: Jesus' Passover with the disciples in the accounts of Matthew, Mark, and Luke, and his call to "'Do this in remembrance of me'" (Luke 22:19). The theology and practice of the Lord's Supper is also fed by stories and themes of the Hebrew Scriptures (the bread of the Passover, manna in the wilderness, the sacrifices of the temple), and developed in other writings of the New Testament (especially Acts and 1 Corinthians).

What ties these events together as sacraments? They are visible (and tangible, taste-able) signs of the grace of God for the body of Christ, directly commended by Jesus and continued by his followers for two millennia. Other rites of the church—confirmation, ordination, weddings, rites at the time of death—have a long history in Christian worship and deep importance in pastoral care and nurture. In some other Christian churches, these are numbered among the sacraments. Indeed, we would affirm that they are closely related to the sacraments, in that confirmation, ordination, the wedding, and the funeral all ripple out from the gift, calling, and promise of our baptism. But for Presbyterians, the only two rites properly called sacraments of the church are Baptism and the Lord's Supper.

26 Why do Presbyterians baptize infants?

A sacrament is a funny thing. It is a gracious act of God, and at the same time, a human response of gratitude. Understanding this little bit of sacramental theology helps us to understand the difference between infant and believer's baptism—and, more importantly, to understand how they can still be one and the same sacrament.

We baptize infants because God chooses, claims, and calls us long before we are able to respond to God's grace. The baptism of infants thus emphasizes God's gracious action, underscoring classic Reformed teaching about "election," how God chooses us for salvation.

We baptize believers (who have not already been baptized) upon the profession of their faith because God's gracious action calls for our grateful response. The baptism of believers thus emphasizes our response to God's grace, demonstrating the central Reformed tenet of salvation by grace through faith.

Seven words from the New Testament sum it up perfectly: "We love because [God] first loved us" (1 John 4:19). God loves us first. There is nothing we can do to earn God's grace. It is a pure gift of love, unexpected and undeserved. This is why we baptize infants. But because God first loves us, we love. Because of the great love of God poured into our hearts, we are able to love God and one another. This is our grateful response to God's grace, our faithful response to God's faithfulness. And this is why we baptize believers upon profession of their faith.

Sometimes people are presented for baptism who do not fall neatly into one of these categories. Examples include children between the ages of infancy and adolescence or people with cognitive disabilities. This is when it is critical to remember that there are not really two kinds of baptism; there is but one sacrament practiced in different ways, depending on the age and situation of the one baptized. In these cases, pastors and elders must work with families and candidates for baptism to discern which practice is most appropriate—relying, as always, on the grace and love of God. Indeed, it is on this grace and love alone that our salvation truly depends.

27 What is the baptismal formula? Why those words?

According to the final words of the Gospel of Matthew, Jesus gave this commission to his disciples after he rose from the dead: "'All authority in heaven and on earth has been given to me. Go therefore and make disciples of all nations, baptizing them in the name of the Father and of the Son and of the Holy Spirit, and teaching them to obey everything that I have commanded you. And remember, I am with you always, to the end of the age'" (Matt. 28:18–20).

These are the words of institution said in the sacrament of baptism, just as we repeat Jesus' commandment "Do this in remembrance of me" at the Lord's Supper. In keeping with Jesus' great commission, when we welcome a new member into Christ's body, we do so with water and the name of the triune God: Father, Son, and Holy Spirit. Though there may have been exceptions to this formula in the early church, and there continue to be variations in the baptismal liturgy, this has been the predominant practice of Christian churches and probably will be "to the end of the age."

The use of this Trinitarian baptismal formula means that when we are claimed by God through the sacrament of baptism, we are marked, signed, or sealed with God's own holy, triune name. It is like the revelation of God's name to Moses at the burning bush: "I AM WHO I AM" (Exod. 3:14). Because we are baptized, who we are is now inextricably linked to who God is. We are immersed in the eternal life and abundant love of the Trinity, one God in three persons—a "community" of mutuality, relationship, and self-giving; a communion of goodness, grace, and glory.

"Father, Son, and Holy Spirit" came to have a special place as an orthodox expression of the divine name, one consistent with the imagery of Scripture and the teachings of the church. Yet there are many other ways—both ancient and contemporary—to describe and contemplate the mystery of the triune God: Speaker, Word, and Breath; Font, Water, and River; Table, Food, and Server; Mother, Child, and Womb; Giver, Gift, and Giving; Lover, Beloved, and Love. It is critical that we expand our Trinitarian vocabulary with these and other expressions, as the exclusive use of "Father, Son, and Holy Spirit" has reflected and contributed to the problem of oppressive patriarchy in the church and can be traumatizing for those who have been abused by men.

At the same time, significant ecumenical relationships, including the 2013 Catholic/Reformed mutual recognition of baptism, are established on this baptismal wording. Therefore, our Directory for Worship says, "As there is one body, there is one Baptism. The Presbyterian Church (U.S.A.) recognizes all baptisms by other Christian churches that are administered with water and performed in the name of the triune God—Father, Son, and Holy Spirit" (*Book of Order*, W-3.0402). How can we reconcile the hope of Christian unity with the concern for more expansive language in worship? The "Riverside Formula," so named for its origin at the Riverside Church in New York City, offers a creative and graceful solution: "N., I baptize you in the name of the Father, and of the Son, and of the Holy Spirit, one God, Mother of us all."

28 Sprinkling, pouring, immersion . . . is there a right way to baptize?

The minimal requirements for a valid baptism are the use of water and the name of the Trinity. The water may be applied with the pastor's hand, poured out from a shell or vessel, or delivered through total immersion in a baptismal pool. Any one of these options is a legitimate form of baptism, according to the Presbyterian Directory for Worship (see *Book of Order*, W-3.0407). The question is, How do we best convey the grace of the Lord Jesus Christ, the love of God, and the communion of the Holy Spirit?

The 1982 World Council of Churches' study *Baptism, Eucharist, and Ministry* offered a set of five theological themes related to baptism, held in common across various Christian traditions. These themes include dying and rising with Christ; cleansing, pardon, and renewal; the gift of the Holy Spirit; incorporation into the body; and the sign of the realm of God. Let's consider the first three of these themes as they relate to the water used in the sacrament of baptism.

If baptism is dying and rising with Christ, what use of water might reflect that experience? Certainly a dangerous amount, enough to drown in and emerge gasping with gratitude for life made new.

If baptism is cleansing, pardon, and renewal, what use of water might suggest that meaning? Certainly a healthy serving, enough to wash away the stain of sin and stench of death.

If baptism is the gift of the Holy Spirit, what use of water might demonstrate that conviction? Certainly a generous portion, enough to fill our hearts with love, joy, peace, patience, kindness, generosity, faithfulness, gentleness, and self-control.

According to Scripture, the grace of God overflows for us through Christ Jesus, who "came into the world to save sinners" (1 Tim. 1:14–15). No amount of water will be sufficient to express this extravagant gift of grace. But a more generous use of water—whether applied through sprinkling, pouring, or immersion—will help to draw worshipers into the deeper mystery and meaning of the sacrament.

29 Can I be rebaptized?

As noted above, sacraments are both gracious acts of God and human responses to God's grace. To suggest that someone who has already been baptized might need to be baptized again is to forget or deny the first part of this premise. Baptism is God's action—and God doesn't mess up. God doesn't miss.

Even—or especially—in our weakness and wavering, our failure and fear, our struggle and sin, God's grace is sufficient for us (2 Cor. 12:9). As the Directory for Worship puts it, "God's faithfulness to us is sure, even when human faithfulness to God is not" (*Book of Order*, W-3.0402). It is true that we make promises in baptism; but in the baptismal covenant God also makes promises, and the word of God stands forever. Thus the Directory for Worship makes it plain: "Baptism is not repeated" (W-3.0402).

There are many opportunities for the reaffirmation of baptism. The profession of faith (or confirmation), ordination and installation, weddings, services of wholeness, and even the Christian funeral are pastoral occasions that "flow from the font," life passages that spring from the sacrament of baptism. This is why the oil of anointing, a repeatable part of the baptismal liturgy, is appropriately applied at such services and why they may include other elements in common with the rite of baptism, such as presentations, questions, the giving of a new garment, or the exchange of symbolic gifts. We also reaffirm our baptism whenever we witness the baptism of another member of the body of Christ, when new people join the church, and each time we share in the Lord's Supper. All of these events are a chance to "remember your baptism and be thankful."

"But what if I don't remember my baptism?" Indeed, this is the reason some request to be rebaptized—they were baptized as infants and have no recollection of the event. The point of this common liturgical phrase is not to remember *when* you *were* baptized but to remember *that* you *are* baptized. Such requests may present good opportunities for the reaffirmation of baptism as a sign of growth in faith or for a discussion of baptismal discipleship in the context of pastoral care. The gift and grace of baptism doesn't depend on the strength of our memory, thanks be to God.

The important thing is this: God remembers. As Paul wrote to the Philippians, "I am confident of this, that the one who began a good work among you will bring it to completion by the day of Jesus Christ" (Phil. 1:6).

30 What is the difference between the Lord's Supper, the Eucharist, and Communion?

Each of these terms may be appropriately applied to the church's ancient practice of sharing bread and wine in Jesus' name. However, each term highlights a different facet of the meaning of the feast and can therefore be helpful in expanding our understanding of the sacrament.

Lord's Supper, particularly prominent in Presbyterian/Reformed tradition, emphasizes Christ's institution of the sacrament and connects the meal with its celebration on the Lord's Day (Sunday). A danger of this term is that it can be easily conflated and confused with "Last Supper"—itself a misnomer since Jesus shared other meals with his followers after he rose from the dead and continues to set a table for us to this day. While we trace Christ's institution of the sacrament to his Passover with the disciples, the meaning of *Lord's Supper* is not exhausted by that event but includes Jesus' feeding of the multitude and his resurrection meals. If *Lord's Supper* equals "Last Supper," every communion Sunday feels like Maundy Thursday—a limited experience of the sacrament indeed.

Eucharist, from a Greek word meaning "to give thanks," emphasizes the essential nature of the sacrament as an offering of thanksgiving for the gift of God's grace in Jesus Christ. This term tends to have more currency in ecumenical and Roman Catholic discussion. A drawback of this word is that it takes some unpacking and may strike some worshipers as esoteric or obscure. The word is worth the work for us, however, as it underscores a sometimes-neglected theological theme: that of gratitude.

Holy Communion refers to a specific part of the eucharistic liturgy—the sharing of bread and wine—and a particular aspect of its theological meaning—the spiritual fellowship of the body of Christ. Over time and in some circles, however, this term has come to stand in for the sacrament as a whole. A potential hazard of this term, once again, is that it may narrow the horizons of the meal, emphasizing only one part of its theology and practice.

Small wonder, then, that the church has developed a variety of terms for this sharing in the body and blood of Christ—it truly is a feast of meaning and mystery.

31 What's the least we have to do for a valid celebration of Communion?

Instead of asking, "What's the least we have to do for the sacrament to 'count'?" why not ask, "What's the most we might do to glorify God and nourish God's people?" Instead of settling for validity, why not strive for vibrancy, search for variety, and stretch for vitality in Christian worship?

Even though the question is troubling, the impulse behind it is understandable. Pastors and congregations may be interested in celebrating the sacrament more frequently but worry that this will involve a lengthy and complicated eucharistic liturgy, perhaps because that's the only thing they have ever experienced. So let's get back to basics.

The sacraments can be said to consist of words from God, joined with actions of the church, surrounded by prayer. (This is true for baptism as well as the Lord's Supper.) All three—words, actions, and prayer—are essential elements of the eucharistic liturgy as described in the Presbyterian Directory for Worship (*Book of Order*, W-3.0411–14). We'll look briefly at each.

First, the words. The words of institution (see Matt. 26; Mark 14; Luke 22; and 1 Cor. 11) are to be used at some point in the eucharistic liturgy. The Presbyterian tradition provides three options: (1) at the invitation to the table, (2) during the Great Thanksgiving, or (3) at the breaking of the bread. The first option reflects an older Reformed tradition, explaining why we "do this." The second represents a common ecumenical practice, though one that is new to many Presbyterians. And the third seems to be the most familiar pattern in Presbyterian churches today. For a host of reasons, many churches are exploring the second option. It facilitates the celebration of a joyful feast, offers a fresh perspective on the sacrament, frames the words of institution with thankful prayer, and strengthens ecumenical relationships, among other things. Just remember that the bread is still broken (and the cup is poured) *after* the prayer, in silence or with other appropriate words of Jesus.

Second, the action. The central action is breaking bread, a phrase sometimes used as a synonym for the sacrament in the New Testament and early church. The breaking of the bread is a symbolic action with many layers of meaning. It is connected with the abundance of Jesus' life, as in the miraculous multiplication of loaves; with the agony of his death, as in the crucifixion of his body and the shedding of his blood; and with the awe of his resurrection, as in the eyes that were opened at the breaking of the bread. The act of breaking bread occurs within the fourfold action of "taking, blessing, breaking, giving" described repeatedly in the Gospels— at Jesus' feeding of the crowds, the meal in the upper room, and on the day of resurrection. This fourfold pattern corresponds to the four-part shape of the whole eucharistic liturgy: Offering (taking), Great Thanksgiving (blessing), Breaking of the Bread (breaking), and Communion (giving).

Third, the prayer. The Great Thanksgiving or eucharistic prayer has a Trinitarian shape, consisting of thanksgiving to God, remembrance of Jesus Christ, and prayer for the Holy Spirit. Within this threefold pattern, key elements include thanks and praise for the gift of God's saving love in the story of Scripture and in our own lives; self-offering to God in the name of Jesus Christ, crucified, risen, and coming again to glory; and calling on the power of the Holy Spirit to nourish us in Christ's body and blood and send us out to share God's grace with others. Please take note—this prayer is called the Great Thanksgiving, not the "long thanksgiving." It is great because it is the great Table prayer of the church, our way of "saying grace" at the meal Christ prepares. It should be theologically full, including the basic elements described here, but doesn't need to be all that long. Indeed, the 2018 *Book of Common Worship* provides examples of strong and fulsome eucharistic prayers that are shorter than this paragraph.

32 What are the proper Communion elements?

Just as the sacraments are divine actions and human responses, the elements used in the Lord's Supper are gifts of God's creation refined and prepared through the work of human hands. Grain is harvested, flour is milled, leaven is added, loaves are kneaded, bread is baked. Vines are plucked, grapes are crushed, juice is strained, wine is fermented, barrels are aged. These are the gifts of God for the people of God.

The eucharistic elements represent the full dimensions of our human experience. Bread is common food, simple fare, ordinary nourishment—as in "our daily bread." Wine or grape juice is a strong, sweet, or special drink—reserved for times of celebration.

When it comes to sacramental matter, cultural context matters. The bread may be made from corn, rice, wheat, or some other grain that is authentic and appropriate for a particular community of faith. The same considerations apply for the cup. The preparation and presentation of the elements offer another way to reflect cultural context. Whatever elements are used and however they are prepared, care should be taken to connect them with Jesus' use of these symbols in saying, "'I am the bread of life'" (John 6:35) and "'I am the vine, you are the branches'" (John 15:5).

Planners and leaders of worship must also take care to provide for the full participation of all, including those who have allergies, addictions, or other dietary restrictions. Some of these concerns are easy enough to anticipate—nonalcoholic and gluten-free options, for instance. Other issues will require regular consultation and pastoral knowledge of the particular needs of the congregation and its members. The options provided for participating in Communion must be clearly identified and communicated to worshipers, including first-time or occasional visitors.

Careful consideration of all these matters will help to ensure that the elements for Communion really are gifts of God for the people of God.

33 Is there a right way to serve and receive Communion?

As with the administration of baptism, there are various options for serving Communion: plates passed through the congregation, intinction (in which a piece of bread is dipped into the cup), or the sharing of a common loaf and chalice. Furthermore, our Directory for Worship provides for various kinds of congregational participation in the sacrament: going forward to the chancel, remaining seated in the sanctuary, or gathering together around a table (*Book of Order*, W-3.0414). Whatever the manner of distribution, the important thing is that the sacrament is *gracefully* served and *gratefully* received.

Those who serve Communion (whether ruling elders or others approved by the session to do so) should be prepared to serve the elements *gracefully*. This means attending prayerfully to the congregation as members of the body of Christ—not rushing through the motions or becoming overly anxious about the logistics. It means making eye contact and connecting with those you serve. It means adopting a peaceful and joyful demeanor and a deep sense of generosity, kindness, and humility. You don't need to wear a cheesy grin or a sorrowful grimace. You're not serving hors d'oeuvres at a cocktail party or administering medicine at an infirmary. You're sharing the grace of Jesus Christ, the love of God, and the communion of the Holy Spirit.

The congregation should be formed in such a way as to receive the elements *gratefully*. This means attending prayerfully to the ones serving as ministers in Christ's name—not checking your watch or grumbling about the long line to the chancel. It means making eye contact and connecting with those who are serving you. It means reflecting on the generosity of God and offering your life to the Lord as a sign of thanks and praise. You don't need to put on a spiritual show or a pious pretense. You're not getting a treat for good behavior or a vaccination at the pharmacy. You're receiving the grace of Jesus Christ, the love of God, and the communion of the Holy Spirit.

In actual practice, the roles of serving and receiving often blend together. This is the case when plates are passed through the congregation or when the bread and cup are shared around a circle. In these situations, the receivers become the servers for the next person. It is especially important in these situations to model graceful serving and grateful receiving.

The act of Communion makes the most sense when we receive the bread from the hand of another person. God's grace comes to us as a gift, not something we grasp and take for ourselves like candy from a bowl. A better practice is to extend your hands to the server, palms open, one cupped in the other. The server places the bread in your hand, saying, "The bread of heaven" or "The body of Christ," and you respond, "Amen" or "Thanks be to God." (This is also a more sanitary method of distribution than having everyone in line touch the bread.)

When it is practiced prayerfully, as an act of grace and gratitude, the giving and receiving of Communion can be one of the most significant spiritual disciplines in the life of a congregation. Those serving the sacrament have the profound opportunity to embody the Lord of service and love within the community of faith. Those receiving it are nourished by the bread of life as they learn to love and serve others in the world around us.

34 How often should we celebrate Communion?

Word and sacrament belong together in the life of the church. As our *Book of Confessions* and *Book of Order* affirm, the church is defined by the proclamation of the Word, the celebration of the sacraments, and a disciplined life in covenant community (see Scots Confession 3.18 and Form of Government F-1.0303). When we gather for worship each Sunday, we should practice these elements of our common life and show forth these signs to the world.

Contrary to popular thought, weekly Eucharist is hardly a new idea for churches of the Reformed tradition. John Calvin called for the Lord's Supper to be "set before the church very often, and at least once a week" (*Institutes* 4.17.43). Commenting on Acts 2:42, Calvin observed that among the earliest Christians "it became the unvarying rule that no meeting of the church should take place without the Word, prayers, partaking of the Supper, and almsgiving" (*Institutes* 4.14.44).

Accordingly, our Directory for Worship says, "The Lord's Supper shall be celebrated as a regular part of the Service for the Lord's Day, preceded by the proclamation of the Word, in the gathering of the people of God. When local circumstances call for the Lord's Supper to be celebrated less frequently, the session may approve other schedules for celebration, in no case less than quarterly" (*Book of Order*, W-3.0409).

Many congregations currently celebrate the Lord's Supper on the first Sunday of the month. While this represents a significant improvement over the quarterly services of previous generations, it is a curious pattern—one without much biblical, theological, or historical grounding. A stronger case can be made for celebrating the Lord's Supper each Lord's Day, as a feast with the risen Christ. After all, the Gospels don't tell us that Jesus rose from the dead on the first Sunday of the month but on the first day of the week.

Granted, local circumstances may make this pattern of celebration difficult. Some congregations have a hard time finding and
retaining leaders who are ordained and equipped to preside at
Table. Thus the Directory for Worship continues, "If the Lord's
Supper is celebrated less frequently than on each Lord's Day,
public notice is to be given at least one week in advance so that all
may prepare to receive the Sacrament" (W-3.0409).

35 Won't weekly Communion be less special?

Yes and no.

On the one hand, seeing the Lord's Supper as something less
"special"—as in occasional, unusual, or out of the ordinary—
would be a good thing for many congregations. The celebration
of the Eucharist is supposed to be one of the defining features of
Christian life and marks of the church. For many Christians around
the world and throughout much of our history this has been the
case. We ought to experience the Lord's Supper as an ordinary
feature of the Service for the Lord's Day, an integral part of what
we do when we gather for worship in Jesus' name.

On the other hand, the practice of celebrating the Eucharist on
a regular basis will help us to appreciate how truly special it is—a
feast of gratitude for the grace of Jesus Christ, an offering of nourishment from the love of God, and an experience of communion
in the Holy Spirit. If we really understood and appreciated what
a gift Christ has given us in the Lord's Supper, we would want to
gather for this meal as often as possible!

Think of the manna God showered upon the people of Israel
each day as they journeyed through the wilderness. On one hand, a
thing so simple, so ordinary—daily bread, a fine flaky substance as
common as the morning dew; on the other, a thing so amazing, so
extraordinary—bread from heaven, the life-saving, life-sustaining
grace and providence of God. This is what the Lord's Supper
should be, and indeed what it becomes for those who make this
meal a regular part of the practice of worship.

36 Does the Communion liturgy have to be so long?

Not necessarily. With a little planning and coordination (as should be the norm in any service, right?) the liturgy for the Lord's Supper can be relatively simple and succinct.

As congregations are celebrating the Eucharist more frequently, it isn't necessary for the Great Thanksgiving to cover the whole story of salvation in every service. Eucharistic prayers may focus on the stories and themes of the texts for the day, the seasons and festivals of the Christian year, and the particular celebrations and concerns of the community of faith. Recent service books such as the 2018 *Book of Common Worship* offer many models for eucharistic prayers that have a strong Trinitarian structure, theological content, and biblical imagery—even with fewer words.

At the same time, congregations should celebrate the Eucharist in a way that is unapologetically rich and full, a feast of God's grace. Everyone has a part to play in such celebration. Musicians can lead lively, engaging congregational songs to draw worshipers into the celebration of this joyful meal. Pastors can preside at the table with gestures that embody "great thanksgiving" and fervent prayer. Communion servers can share the bread and cup in a way that conveys the deep love and humble service of Christ. Worshipers can devote themselves to the contemplation of the great mystery of our faith.

In planning for a complete and concise Service for the Lord's Day, it helps to have a clear sense of the big picture and overall flow of the order of worship. Think of the Word as the first half of the service, beginning with the gathering, and the Eucharist as the second half, concluding with the sending. Then pace and proportion the various elements of the liturgy accordingly. Worship planners might find other ways to trim time from the service—eliminating unnecessary announcements, avoiding long explanations of the liturgy, and eschewing ornamental elements that don't serve to promote the people's participation in prayer and praise.

And if the service runs a little longer than usual, what's so wrong with that? Time in the presence of God and the communion of saints—preparing for an eternity of worship around God's throne—is time well spent. Worshipers might be a little late for lunch, but they'll be a little early for the heavenly banquet to come.

6

The Christian Year

 What is the most important day of the liturgical year?

Sunday. There are surprisingly few events in the life of Jesus about which the four Gospels speak unanimously. One of those key details is that he rose from the dead early in the morning on the first day of the week. In keeping with this clear witness from the evangelists, for two millennia Christians have gathered on Sunday to celebrate the resurrection of Jesus Christ. We have come to call this the Lord's Day—a name that also evokes the prophets' longing for the coming "day of the Lord."

Because of the centrality of Christ's dying, rising, and promised return, the pattern of the week is of primary importance in Christian timekeeping. Each Sunday encapsulates the great mystery of faith: "Christ has died, Christ is risen, Christ will come again."

Christians have other ways of marking time through the day and through the year, but the weekly celebration of the Lord's Day is the primary pulse or cadence of our common life. Consider two musical analogies. Think of a song in 7/8 time. The rhythm of the Lord's Day is synchronized with the Jewish practice of Sabbath keeping, but it puts the accent on a different beat—the first day of creation instead of the seventh. Or think of a musical scale. The Lord's Day is much like the eighth note (octave) of a seven-tone scale—completing the cycle of the week and marking the beginning of God's new creation. Indeed, the Lord's Day is sometimes called the "eighth day of the week" or the "eighth day of creation."

Beyond the pattern of the week, there are two cycles of time in the Christian year (see below), each centered around a great festival day: the Nativity of the Lord (or Christmas) and the Resurrection of the Lord (or Easter). Note that these key festivals correspond with central doctrines of the Christian faith: the incarnation and resurrection of Jesus Christ. Each season of celebration ends with a culminating festival: Epiphany for Christmas and Pentecost for Easter.

There are a number of other significant festival days throughout the Christian year, mostly associated with events in the life of Christ (as in the Baptism, Transfiguration, and Ascension of the Lord) or doctrines of Christian faith (as in Trinity Sunday and Christ the King / Reign of Christ Sunday). Ash Wednesday is a call to repentance and reconciliation at the beginning of the season of Lent. All Saints' Day is a commemoration of all the faithful people of God throughout history and can be a time to remember those who have died in the past year. Holy Week is an intensive annual immersion in the story of Christ's death and resurrection, beginning with Palm/Passion Sunday and concluding with the Three Days (Maundy Thursday, Good Friday, and the Easter Vigil). Various Christian traditions also observe other days, such as the Holy Name of Jesus (January 1), the Presentation of the Lord (February 2), the Annunciation of the Lord (March 25), the Visitation of Mary to Elizabeth (May 31), Holy Cross (September 14), and Reformation Day (October 31).

All of time is created by God, redeemed by Christ, and made holy by the Spirit (see *Book of Order*, W-1.0201). We are called to pray, watch, and be ready at all times for the coming of the day of the Lord. Thus, in another sense, we might say that the most important day of the liturgical year is . . . today.

38 What are the seasons of the Christian year?

The Christian year consists of four seasons—not winter, spring, summer, and fall but Advent, Christmas, Lent, and Easter. To understand how we came to have these four seasons and how they are related to one another and to the rest of the liturgical calendar, it might be helpful to take a very brief excursion through two thousand years of church history.

From the earliest centuries of Christian worship to the present day, the primary festivals of the Christian year have been those that proclaim the two pivotal doctrines of the faith—incarnation and resurrection. The annual commemoration of the death and resurrection of the Lord at Easter (or Pascha) came first, as is evident in sources from the second century; after much controversy, in the year 325 the Council of Nicaea established the formula for calculating the date of this springtime festival according to the phases of the moon. The development of an annual celebration of the nativity of the Lord followed, with Christmas established on December 25 by the fourth century in Rome.

Throughout the next few hundred years, around these primary Christian festivals grew up two cycles, together consisting of four seasons. The Easter cycle is centered on the resurrection of the Lord and includes Lent, a six-week, forty-day season of preparation (actually forty-six days, including Sundays); and Easter, a seven-week, fifty-day season of celebration. Similarly, the Christmas cycle is centered on the nativity of the Lord and includes Advent, its own four-week season of preparation, and Christmas, a twelve-day season of celebration.

In between these cycles, the church has another way of keeping time—focusing on the weekly preparation for and celebration of the resurrection of the Lord. We sometimes call this "ordinary time," from a Latin root referring to Sundays in order. The first (and shorter) segment of ordinary time occurs after Epiphany, between the end of Christmas and the beginning of Lent. This period of time is framed by festivals celebrating the baptism and transfiguration of the Lord (observances that can be traced to the early centuries of Christian history but held on differing dates throughout the ecumenical church). The second (and much longer) span of ordinary time occurs after Pentecost, between the end of Easter and the beginning of the new Christian year at Advent. This period of time is framed by Trinity Sunday (established in the fourteenth century) and Christ the King (established in 1925).

All of these cycles, seasons, and festivals help us to contemplate and celebrate key affirmations of Christian faith—namely, the incarnation and resurrection of the Lord and everything that surrounds and stems from them. They provide a way for us to inhabit these great mysteries so that they might shape our faith and change our lives. Just as the natural world around us is transformed through the rhythms of the year, we are called to live and grow and die and rise again as we keep time with Christ.

39 Why does the church year begin with Advent?

A mysterious thing happens in the last few weeks of the calendar year. The Christian understanding and experience of time seems to turn upside down and inside out. Is Advent a beginning or an ending? Are we looking forward or looking back? Or is it somehow all of the above?

Advent means "coming" or "arrival." In the season of Advent we anticipate the coming of the Lord in two ways—first (in the early weeks of Advent), at the end of time in a cloud of glory, and then second (in the later weeks of Advent), two thousand years ago as a child in a manger. At the beginning of the season the question is "What are we waiting for?" We long for the fulfillment of God's promises. We yearn for the day when death is no more and God will wipe away every tear. By the end of the season the question has become "Who are we waiting for?" We are eager to welcome the Word of God made flesh. We are ready to greet the Savior, the Messiah, the Lord.

On the First Sunday of Advent, the Christian year begins with a glimpse of the end—the life of the world to come. The prophets share their vision of God's realm of righteousness, justice, and peace. The apostles teach us to prepare for the coming day of the Lord. Jesus urges us to watch the signs of the times and trust in the promise of his saving love. The lectionary actually previews these themes in the final three weeks of the Christian year, including Christ the King / Reign of Christ Sunday. This is helpful information for preachers and worship planners seeking to get a head start on Advent before the culture of Christmas snowballs and consumes everything in its path.

By the Fourth Sunday of Advent, the time is ripe for a new beginning—the mystery of the incarnation. The hopes of the prophets are fulfilled in a young woman, great with child. The message of the apostles is about to be revealed. Our watching and waiting have come to an end. Emmanuel—God with us—is on the way. The lectionary features stories of Mary and Joseph as they struggle to comprehend the wondrous new thing God is about to do.

At the beginning of the Christian year we remember, celebrate, and anticipate the work of the Lord God "'who was and is and is to come'" (Rev. 4:8). "'See, I am coming soon,'" says the Lord. "'I am the Alpha and the Omega, the first and the last, the beginning and the end'" (Rev. 22:12–13). Amen. Come, Lord Jesus!

40 What is the history and use of the Advent wreath?

Advent wreaths began as a family devotional practice in Germany, probably around the seventeenth century. As with Advent calendars in Christian homes today, the candles provided a way to mark time as families gathered to read Scripture, sing, and pray through the season. It was only sometime in the mid-twentieth century that the tradition of the Advent wreath made its move from personal prayer into public worship.

The older origins of Advent wreaths are likely to be found in pagan practices around the winter solstice. The increasing light of each candle, framed by a circle of evergreen branches, brought comfort and hope in the shortest, darkest days of the year. This idea of indomitable illumination accords with the Christian affirmation in the coming of Jesus Christ: "The light shines in the darkness, and the darkness did not overcome it" (John 1:5). We find a mirror image of this tradition in the Tenebrae candles of Holy Week.

In common, contemporary use, Advent wreaths typically consist of a ring of four candles (three purple and one pink) with a fifth candle (white) in the center. The pink (or rose) candle is customarily lighted on the Third Sunday of Advent (*Gaudete* Sunday, from the Latin word for "rejoice"). This tradition is related to the idea of the Third Sunday of Advent as an oasis of joy in an otherwise somber season, given the prominence of the word "rejoice" in many of the lectionary texts for the day. Contrary to popular wisdom, the candles aren't intended to be associated with particular biblical characters (such as "shepherds," "magi," etc.) or themes (such as "love," "peace," "hope," etc.). The primary significance of the Advent wreath comes from the image of light growing in darkness; this symbolism is much more important than the colors or themes of particular candles.

Many published liturgical resources provide appropriate sentences of Scripture to accompany the lighting of the Advent candles. The 2018 *Book of Common Worship* suggests verses from Isaiah, since this prophet is so associated with the Advent season and the coming of the Messiah. Worship planners might also wish to use stanzas of an Advent hymn for each week or the selections from ancient "O Antiphons" (perhaps best known through the hymn "O Come, O Come Emmanuel"; see *Glory to God*, no. 88).

41 Why do we have the first Christmas service at night?

In the ancient Jewish/Christian way of keeping liturgical time, there is the understanding that the new day begins at sunset. This notion is reflected in the account of creation at the beginning of the Bible, with its daily refrain "And there was evening and there was morning . . ." (Gen. 1:5, e.g.). In keeping with this chronology, the Jewish Sabbath begins at sunset on Friday, the eve of the seventh day, and ends at nightfall on Saturday.

The primary festivals of the Christian year also reflect this rhythm. We celebrate the first service of the nativity season on

Christmas Eve, December 24. Similarly, the Saturday night Great Vigil of Easter is the first service of the Easter season. We have a special order of worship for other Saturday evenings throughout the year—the Vigil of the Resurrection. (This liturgy offers a good model for congregations interested in starting a Saturday night worship service.) In fact, our whole system of daily prayer is based on this understanding of time. It puts evening prayer before morning, following the pattern of death and resurrection in Christian faith, life, and worship.

Scripture seems to suggest that God's timing favors the evening hours. According to Luke, the shepherds were "keeping watch over their flock by night" (Luke 2:8) when they heard the angels singing of Jesus' coming. Similarly, according to Matthew, the magi followed a star to the place of his birth (Matt. 2:9). According to John, it was "early on the first day of the week, while it was still dark" (John 20:1) when Mary Magdalene discovered that Jesus had risen from the dead. Apparently, preachers aren't the only ones who sometimes pull an all-nighter to proclaim the good news.

42 What is Epiphany?

In common usage, an "epiphany" is a sudden and personal moment of revelation or insight glimpsed in everyday life. In biblical, theological, and liturgical use, however, the Epiphany of the Lord is far from sudden, personal, or "everyday" (as in commonplace).

As the apostle wrote to the Ephesians,

Although I am the very least of all the saints, this grace was given to me to bring to the Gentiles the news of the boundless riches of Christ, and to make everyone see what is the plan of the mystery hidden for ages in God who created all things; so that through the church the wisdom of God in its rich variety might now be made known to the rulers and authorities in the heavenly places. This was in accordance with the eternal purpose that [God] has carried out in Jesus Christ our Lord. (Eph. 3:8–11)

This scriptural quotation offers a summary of all that Epiphany means in Christian faith and worship.

First—far from sudden—Ephesians describes the good news of Epiphany as "the plan of the mystery hidden for ages" and part of the "eternal purpose" of God. The revelation of Jesus Christ as Lord and Savior of all is the culmination of God's providential plan and purpose—the fulfillment of the law, the hope of the prophets, and the redemption of the world.

Second—far from personal—the purpose of Epiphany is "to make *everyone* see" the good news of Jesus Christ. As this passage makes plain, in Jesus Christ God's covenant is not only open to the people of Israel but extended to the Gentiles (or "nations") as well. Now the curtain is drawn back, and the mystery of the ages is revealed to all.

Third—far from everyday—Ephesians depicts Christ's Epiphany in grand and cosmic terms: "boundless riches" and a "rich variety" of wisdom, made known to the "rulers and authorities in the heavenly places." The Epiphany of the Lord has global, even universal implications. This is a story that begins in the everyday life of a child in Bethlehem but reaches out into all the world.

The visual symbolism of Epiphany is often centered around light shining in darkness. The lectionary readings for the day support this theme. Isaiah announces, "Arise, shine; for your light has come, and the glory of the LORD has risen upon you. . . . Nations shall come to your light, and kings to the brightness of your dawn. . . . They shall bring gold and frankincense" (Isa. 60:1, 3, 6). And right on cue, those rulers arrive from afar, following the light of a star to present their precious gifts to the Christ child: "For we observed his star at its rising, and have come to pay him homage" (Matt. 2:2).

The theme of illumination also reflects the prologue to the Gospel of John, read at the Nativity of the Lord: "The light shines in the darkness, and the darkness did not overcome it" (John 1:5). Indeed, the image of light shining in darkness is a "bookend" for the twelve days of the season of Christmas, which begin with the Nativity of the Lord (December 25) and conclude with the

Epiphany of the Lord (January 6). Now the glory of the long-awaited Messiah shines for all the earth to see.

43 Why do we mark people with ashes on Ash Wednesday?

Ashes are an ancient biblical symbol of repentance, sorrow, poverty, and sacrifice. They are connected with the image of dust as a sign of mortality; as God told Adam, "'You are dust, and to dust you shall return'" (Gen. 3:19). When Abraham prepared to advocate for the people of Sodom, he said, "'Let me take it upon myself to speak to the Lord, I who am but dust and ashes'" (Gen. 18:27). When Tamar was raped by Amnon, she put ashes on her face and tore her garments (2 Sam. 13:19). Job's whole ordeal was framed by ashes and dust—immediately after he was afflicted, he "sat among the ashes" (Job 2:8), and at the end of God's speech from the whirlwind, he declared he would "repent in dust and ashes" (Job 42:6). When Jonah gave the people of Nineveh forty days to repent, the king "put on sackcloth, and sat in ashes" (Jonah 3:6). By contrast, God is the one who "raises the poor from the dust, and lifts the needy from the ash heap" (Ps. 113:7; cf. 1 Sam. 2:8). The Spirit of the Lord comes "to bring good news to the oppressed" and "to give them a garland instead of ashes" (Isa. 61:1, 3).

The sign of ashes marks the beginning of the season of Lent. On the day called Ash Wednesday we are marked with ashes, tracing the sign of the cross—the sign of Jesus, who gave his own life for our salvation. At this first service of Lent we face our own mortality, repent of our sin, and commit our lives to the grace of God.

For those who take up special spiritual practices during the season of Lent, Ash Wednesday is the beginning of this intentional period of fasting, service, and prayer. For those who are preparing for baptism at the Great Vigil of Easter, Ash Wednesday might be a time to begin their formation through the catechumenate. In some eras of the church's history, Ash Wednesday was an invitation to penitent sinners to submit themselves to the church's discipline

and be restored to full communion with the body of Christ. It can
still be an opportunity for the church to reach out with humility
and grace to those who are alienated and estranged from its fellowship. For all of us, Ash Wednesday is a call to reconciliation—to
be restored to right relationship with God and one another and to
seek peace in the world God loves.

Traditionally, the ashes for Ash Wednesday are made by burning the palm branches from Palm/Passion Sunday of the previous
year. This is fitting, as the symbols of ashes and palms thus frame
the season of Lent. The ashes of Wednesday also anticipate the
dust of death we face on Good Friday. Nevertheless, with the
prayers of the psalmists and hope of the prophets, we trust that God
will raise us from the ashes and dust.

44 What does "Lent" mean? Why is it forty days long?

The word *Lent* is derived from an old English word for spring; it
may be associated with the "lengthening" of days at this time of
the year. As the days grow longer, Lent can be a time for spiritual
growth through disciplines such as fasting, prayer, and service. As
new life blooms around us, Lent can be a season of preparation for
the celebration of Jesus' resurrection.

In Romance languages, such as Spanish, the word for Lent
means "forty days" (e.g., *cuaresma*). Many biblical stories include
a significant period of forty days—the great flood, Moses at Sinai,
Elijah's journey, Jonah at Nineveh, and Jesus in the wilderness.
The season of Lent is patterned after these forty-day periods as a
time of cleansing, instruction, pilgrimage, repentance, and formation for ministry in Jesus' name.

In the early church the season of Lent was a time of preparation
for baptism. Those anticipating baptism at Easter would spend the
forty days of Lent being formed in the basics of Christian faith,
life, and worship. This is still the case among many Christians who
welcome new believers at the Easter Vigil. It may also serve as a

time for young people in the church to prepare for confirmation and for the whole community of faith to consider their lifelong calling to baptismal discipleship.

Sundays are not counted among the forty days of the Lenten season because every Lord's Day is a celebration of Christ's resurrection on the first day of the week. These weekly "festival days" are a respite from the more somber, penitential tone of Lent. We refer to them as Sundays "in Lent," not Sundays "of Lent." This means there are actually forty-six days—forty days plus the six Sundays—between Ash Wednesday and Holy Saturday, the final day of Lent.

The dates of Lent differ from year to year, depending on the date appointed for the Resurrection of the Lord (or Easter day). In Western tradition, Easter is celebrated on the first Sunday after the first full moon on or after the spring equinox. Lent always begins forty-six days before this on Ash Wednesday.

45 Presbyterians don't celebrate Lent, do they?

The point of Lent is reconciliation. The season of Lent offers the church a chance to rediscover and recommit to this basic theme of the gospel—that nothing can separate us from God's love (Rom. 8:39). Each Lent we remember how God sent Jesus to save us from our sin (John 3:17); to break down the dividing walls of hostility between us (Eph. 2:14); and to bring righteousness, justice, and peace to this hurting world (Isa. 9:7). Lent is an annual opportunity to put into practice the ministry of reconciliation God has entrusted to us through Jesus Christ (2 Cor. 5:19).

The Presbyterian Church (U.S.A.)'s Confession of 1967 has a similar focus on the theme of reconciliation:

> The reconciling work of Jesus was the supreme crisis in the life of humankind. His cross and resurrection become personal crisis and present hope for women and men when the gospel is proclaimed and believed. In this experience, the Spirit brings God's forgiveness to all, moves people to respond in faith,

repentance, and obedience, and initiates new life in Christ. (*Book of Confessions*, 9.21)

Lent confronts us with the crisis and challenge of Christ's cross and calls us to repent and return to the Lord, relying on God's reconciling and redeeming work. In this sense, the themes of Lent are consistent with the deepest instincts of the Reformed theological tradition.

Leaders of the Reformed churches have not always seen it this way—to say the least. The earliest Reformers were harshly critical of the season of Lent. John Calvin referred to Lent as a "superstitious observance" in which pastors perpetuated the illusion that people could somehow serve God, imitate Christ, and curry divine favor through feats of sacrifice and self-denial, such as fasting (*Institutes* 4.12.20). Although Calvin was right to condemn these extreme practices and the misguided theology behind them, this is not the spirit in which most contemporary Presbyterians (and other Christians) observe the Lenten season. Lent is a time to prepare for the celebration of the resurrection, the doctrine at the heart of our faith. It is a time to confess our sin, a hallmark of Reformed worship. It is a time to practice our gratitude for God's grace, a classic theme in Reformed theology. It is a time to "be reconciled to God" (2 Cor. 5:20).

The practice of spiritual disciplines during the season of Lent is not about proving ourselves as spiritual superheroes or groveling for God's grace. It is about growing in faith and drawing closer to God and others—our lifelong calling as disciples of Jesus Christ. Some people find it helpful to give up something as a way of focusing their attention on God; others find it more helpful to take up a new practice, such as prayer or service. Whatever form it might take, an authentic and effective spiritual discipline leads us not into self-imposed suffering and alienation but into fullness of life and deeper relationship with God and others.

After five hundred years of Reformed history, and thanks to recent decades of ecumenical theological dialogue, we may rejoice that many of the theological battles of the sixteenth century are now laid to rest. Perhaps we Presbyterians have even reconciled ourselves with the idea of the season of Lent.

46 Why do people avoid saying "alleluia" in Lent?

At least in some corners of the church, there is a long-standing tradition of not singing or saying the word "alleluia" (from the Hebrew for "praise God") during the season of Lent. This certainly doesn't mean that God is any less worthy of praise during the six weeks before Easter. The tradition comes from an attempt to accent the solemnity and sobriety of this penitential season. It seems out of place to utter an alleluia—so strongly associated with Easter celebration—as the church makes its annual pilgrimage to the cross.

Think of it as a movie sound track, with special musical cues that signal approaching danger or a romantic reunion. The avoidance of alleluias gives Lent a different tone, setting the forty days apart from the sounds and symbols of other seasons—in particular, the resurrection joy of Easter. Or think of it as delayed gratification, like saving your dessert until you've finished your vegetables. The suppression of alleluias during the season of Lent makes them seem all the more delicious when Easter finally arrives.

There have been, in fact, complementary sets of traditions around the season of Easter. Early church leaders forbade the practice of fasting and the posture of kneeling throughout the great fifty days of Easter, as they were also forbidden on Sundays. In this way, the whole season of Easter had its own distinctive character as the "great Sunday" of the Christian year.

The astute reader may be wondering why alleluias would be avoided on the Sundays in Lent if each Sunday is a celebration of Christ's resurrection and not counted among the forty days of the Lenten season. Indeed, if we had a practice of worshiping throughout the week, as in monastic communities, one might make a compelling case for avoiding alleluias Monday through Saturday and allowing them on Sunday. But this is an unlikely scenario for most contemporary churches.

It should be noted that the tradition of eschewing alleluias in Lent makes the most sense when a congregation has a regular, reliable practice of singing (e.g., as a Gospel acclamation) or say-ing (e.g., as a response to the benediction) alleluias in the liturgy. When this is the case, the alleluias are more conspicuous in their absence. Such traditions reveal the value of a consistent order of worship in Christian formation.

At the Transfiguration of the Lord, the final Sunday before Lent, some congregations have a tradition of "locking up" or "burying" their alleluias for the duration of Lent. This practice provides an active way for the children of the church to share in the symbol-ism of the season—making colorful alleluia banners, putting them away at Transfiguration, and helping to retrieve them at the Easter Vigil or on the first Sunday of Easter.

Where this tradition is observed, churches find many other ways to bless God's name throughout the season of Lent. Sundays in Lent may serve as an opportunity to expand our vocabulary of praise, singing,

> "Blessing and glory and wisdom
> and thanksgiving and honor
> and power and might."
>   (Rev. 7:12)

These occasions can also help us cultivate the discipline of grati-tude in all seasons—extolling the Lord at all times (Ps. 34:1) and giving thanks in every circumstance (1 Thess. 5:18)—learning to sing God's praise, even in a minor key.

Is it Palm Sunday or Passion Sunday?

Perhaps we should call it Paradox Sunday. Indeed, the Sixth Sunday in Lent presents us with a paradox—the triumph and tragedy of the cross. On this day we celebrate the blessed one who comes in the name of the Lord, and we also remember how he was cursed and mocked by those he came to save. On this day we remember the agony of Jesus' suffering and death while we celebrate this crucified one as our Lord and God. The liturgy for Palm/Passion Sunday seeks to hold all of these confounding, contradictory themes together in constructive tension as we enter into Holy Week.

Our earliest account of the procession with palms at the opening of Holy Week comes from a Spanish nun named Egeria, who took a pilgrimage to Jerusalem at the end of the fourth century and kept a detailed travel diary. She offers a vivid account of how worshipers walked down from the Mount of Olives, chanting, "Blessed is he who comes . . ." (Matt. 21:9; cf. Ps. 118:26). Egeria makes special note of the participation of children, who carried the palm branches. Children too young to keep up with the procession were themselves carried by their parents.

The long reading of the passion narrative on the final Sunday in Lent seems to have come to us from the Holy Week traditions of the church in Rome. The Gospel account of Jesus' suffering and death was (and still is, in some traditions) chanted by three singers—a tenor voice as narrator, a bass as Jesus, and an alto for other characters in the story. In the medieval period, this evolved from a simple recitation of the passion into a dramatic event.

As Western churches have come to observe it in subsequent centuries, Palm/Passion Sunday combines these themes and practices, juxtaposing the triumphal entry with the tragedy of the cross. This tradition has both practical value and theological wisdom. At a practical level, it accounts for worshipers who choose not to attend mid-week services (such as Good Friday), and thus may never hear the whole story of Christ's crucifixion. In a theological sense, as noted above, it confronts us with the scandal of the gospel—that we crucified the very one God sent to save us, yet even death could not silence God's Word, quench God's Spirit, or thwart God's promise.

From the cross—with all its sorrow, suffering, and shame—has come the good news of salvation. To this paradoxical proclamation, we can only respond, "Thanks be to God."

48 What is the symbolism of palm branches?

The palm frond (leaf) was a symbol of triumph in Roman times, bestowed upon the winners of military or athletic contests. When the people of Jerusalem greet Jesus with palm branches, then, they aren't just grabbing whatever is on hand to express their appreciation. The palms symbolize victory, a fitting tribute for the return of a triumphant king.

Yet there are multiple levels of irony in this scene. The one they greet is not a king in a chariot but a humble man riding on a donkey. He comes not with military might but to establish a reign of peace. His "battle" is ahead of him, and it will seem to end in tragic and crushing defeat. The very crowds who are now crying, "Hosanna" ("Save us") will soon be shouting, "Crucify him!"

The palm tree (*tamar*) already had deep roots in Hebrew Scripture. After leaving Egypt, the people of Israel first camped at a place with seventy palm trees (Exod. 15:27). Deborah, prophet and judge, held court under a palm tree (Judg. 4:5); a palm tree uprooted or cut down symbolizes God's judgment (Isa. 9:14; 19:15). Solomon's temple was decorated with carvings of palm trees on the walls and doors (1 Kgs. 6), and the new temple of Ezekiel's vision is similarly adorned (Ezek. 40–41). The palm tree is used as a simile for the righteous in the Psalms (92:12), the body of the beloved in the Song of Songs (7:7–8), and the glory of Israel in Hosea (9:13).

For the early Christians who suffered under Roman persecution, the symbol of the palm branch took on new significance as a sign of faithfulness and perseverance under the threat of death. In Revelation, the white-robed multitude of the redeemed from every tribe and nation, "'they who have come out of the great ordeal'" (Rev. 7:14), wave their palm branches around the throne of God, crying out,

> "Salvation belongs to our God
>   who is seated on the
>   throne, and to the Lamb!"
>   (Rev. 7:10)

In the first few centuries of the church, palms were strongly connected with martyrdom and were sometimes engraved on the tombs of those who died for their convictions.

When we take up palm branches in Holy Week, we take part in this whole holy history. We are a pilgrim people, seeking shelter in the wilderness. We stand under the word and judgment of the Lord. We long to enter the temple of God's presence, to know the righteousness, love, and glory of the Holy One. We chant and cheer with the crowds in the streets of Jerusalem—even as they wonder what to make of this strange Savior. We weep with the victims of violence and oppression in every place. We rejoice with the redeemed as they celebrate God's saving work.

49 Why are there so many services in Holy Week?

Well, it depends on how you count them. At the heart of Holy Week—and the whole Christian year—is a great three-day event celebrating the mystery of our faith in the crucified and risen Lord: the *Triduum* (Latin for "three days"). This is really intended to be *one* service spanning three days, although we often mistakenly think of it as three separate events: Maundy Thursday, Good Friday, and the Great Vigil of Easter. Liturgically speaking, this is evident in the fact that there is no benediction until the end of the Easter Vigil. From a theological perspective, the unity of the Three Days reflects the necessity of holding Christ's life, death, and resurrection together.

The name Maundy Thursday comes from the Latin word *mandatum*, meaning "commandment." On this night we remember Christ's new commandment to love one another as he loves us. This love is expressed in action through foot washing and the Communion meal we share. The washing of feet is a sign of deep love and humble service. Jesus washes his disciples' feet to demonstrate how they are called to love and serve others. In some communities, leaders will be the ones washing feet; in others, people take turns washing the feet of one another. The eucharistic meal recalls Christ's institution of the sacrament at the time of the Passover and provides another opportunity to serve one another in Jesus' name.

On Good Friday we remember the crucifixion and death of Jesus. The service focuses on the proclamation of the passion narrative, with an extended reading from the Gospel of John. It also includes a great prayer of intercession, for the church and the world God loves, and the Solemn Reproaches, Christ's powerful lament from the cross. We call this Friday "good" because of the paradox or irony at the heart of the gospel—that by the grace of God in Jesus Christ, life comes from death; salvation, from suffering; triumph, from tragedy; and good news, from bad. The one who is lifted up on the cross to die will rise from the dust to give us life.

At the Great Vigil of Easter we do just about everything that is possible to do in Christian worship—gathering around a fire, remembering the story of salvation, welcoming new members or reaffirming baptism, and sharing the joyful meal of the risen Lord. Where it is celebrated with creativity and care, the Easter Vigil can be a transforming spiritual experience, a lively intergenerational event, and an engaging feast for all the senses.

In fact, this could be said of the Three Days as a whole. Worship committees are advised to plan these events together, as a single service in three parts. Find ways to weave threads through the Three Days—common leadership, a single worship guide, repeated music, artwork that grows or changes, and creative uses of liturgical space. Involve as many people as possible in planning and leadership—children of the church, Sunday school classes, confirmation cohorts, youth groups, college students on spring break, adult study groups, retired members, deacons, ruling elders, and other pastors in the congregation. Collaborate with other congregations in your community to host these events together, whether with other Presbyterian churches or ecumenical partners.

Instead of thinking of Holy Week as a series of appointments on the church calendar, think of it as something like an annual retreat—an opportunity to renew yourself in the mystery of our faith, to reacquaint yourself with the heart of the gospel, and to rededicate yourself to the service of the crucified and risen Lord. This is the purpose of the great Three Days.

50 Should we have a Christian Seder?

No. The Jewish Seder (from a Hebrew word meaning "order," as in order of worship) is a ritual meal held at the beginning of Passover. The practice of holding a "Christian Seder" service is biblically ambiguous, historically questionable, theologically problematic, liturgically confusing, and potentially offensive to Jewish neighbors. Here's why.

First, the four Gospels present a somewhat different chronology for the week of Jesus' arrest and death. Matthew, Mark, and Luke have him sharing a Passover meal with his disciples. John, however, describes a meal *before* the Passover (John 13:1), with the Passover itself coinciding with Jesus' crucifixion.

Second, it is impossible—highly speculative at best—to reconstruct an authentic order of worship for a first-century Passover meal. The oldest Jewish Seder services come from the ninth century of the Common Era—separated by the better part of a millennium from Jesus' time. Besides this, attempts at historical reenactment in worship tend to undermine the experience of a real encounter with the living God.

Third, to focus on the memory of the exodus is to miss the point of the Lord's Supper, which is, above all, about the liberating and transforming work of God in the life, death, resurrection, and return of Jesus Christ. To be sure, these events are connected and related in the great story of salvation, but the imagery of the exodus has more in common with our passage through the waters of baptism.

Fourth, the Christian Eucharist is its own kind of ritual meal, with a particular form of prayer (the Great Thanksgiving) and a distinctive pattern of action (offering, blessing, breaking, and sharing). To overlay the pattern of the Jewish Seder does a disservice to both orders of worship.

Fifth, Christian Seder services typically seek to adapt the Jewish liturgy by adding distinctively Christian elements, such as the words of institution or Trinitarian doxologies. This misappropriation of a religious ritual may be offensive to Jews. Christians who wish to learn more about the Seder should consult a local rabbi or (if invited) attend the Passover meal as a guest in the home of a Jewish neighbor.

Instead of trying to invent a Christian Seder, worship planners would be better advised to keep the ancient "Christian Passover" celebrated in the Great Vigil of Easter, our annual feast of liberation in Christ. Better yet, immerse your congregation in the mystery of faith and story of salvation by observing the great Three Days (Maundy Thursday, Good Friday, and Easter Vigil) as a single service in three parts.

51 Why is there a fifty-day season of Easter?

"Easter Sunday" is a bit of a misnomer. One day out of 365 is hardly sufficient to celebrate the good news of the gospel—that Christ is risen from the dead. Accordingly, the season of Easter lasts seven weeks, spanning the fifty days from the Resurrection of the Lord to the Day of Pentecost. Thus there are, in fact, *eight* "Easter Sundays."

The notion of Easter as a season of fifty days is patterned after the ancient Jewish festival of seven weeks that extended from the beginning of the barley harvest (on the second day after the beginning of Passover) to the end of the wheat harvest, at the Festival of Weeks (see Deut. 16:9–12). The Festival of Weeks later came to be called Pentecost ("fiftieth day") by Greek-speaking Jews.

In addition to the agricultural calendar, the symbolic value of numbers plays a meaningful role in the duration of this festival. In Hebraic thought, the number seven implies wholeness or completion. Thus there are seven days in a week, the time required for the completion of creation. A period of seven weeks, each consisting of seven days, suggests fullness "squared." The season of Easter is, therefore, a "week" of weeks. Furthermore, seven weeks is roughly one-seventh of a year (fifty-two weeks). Just as Christians set apart one day in seven—the Lord's Day—to celebrate Christ's resurrection, we set apart one-seventh of the year for this season of new life.

The number fifty also has symbolic significance, since Leviticus 25 designates every fiftieth year as a time of jubilee, when captives are to be released and debts are to be forgiven. Easter, as a season of fifty days, represents the "great jubilee," in which we are released from captivity to death and the debt of our sin is forgiven by God.

Finally, in an eschatological sense, the Day of Pentecost stands just outside, but adjacent to, the "week" of weeks (forty-nine days) as the great fiftieth day. Just as Sunday is considered the "eighth day" of creation, since Christ rose from the dead on the first day of the week, Pentecost is the culmination or completion of the Easter season and a day of new creation in the Christian year.

Hidden within the fifty days of Easter is a span of forty days— the time between the Resurrection and Ascension of the Lord, celebrated on the sixth Thursday of Easter. While this time is not observed as a season in itself, it corresponds to the forty days of Jesus' appearances to the disciples after rising from the dead (Acts 1:3) and stands as a kind of echo or reflection of the season of Lent.

52 Is ordinary time "ordinary"?

Let's consider this question from the theological perspective of a third-grader—with a head full of Bible stories, a heart full of children's songs, and a handful of crayons (purple, gold, red, and green).

When one surveys the circle of the Christian year, it is evident that the Christmas and Easter cycles (with the shorter period of ordinary time between them) occupy about half of the calendar. The remainder of the year consists of the much longer period of ordinary time. As we experience the Christian year, it does feel as though the first half is packed with special traditions, liturgical action, seasonal music, and changing colors, while the second half of the year just stretches out . . . Sunday by Sunday by Sunday.

So, is ordinary time more "ordinary"? The answer is yes and no. There is a sense in which these periods of time in the liturgical calendar fall outside the seasons of prayerful preparation (Advent and Lent) and joyful celebration (Christmas and Easter) that fill the Christian year with so much of its pathos and excitement, poignancy and exultation. Yet, in another sense, the weekly rhythm of ordinary time is a chance to prepare for and celebrate Jesus' resurrection on the Lord's Day—the faith-shaping, life-changing, world-shaking mystery of his dying and rising. And there's nothing ordinary about that.

The name for ordinary time isn't intended to imply that these Sundays are commonplace, routine, or mundane. It comes from the idea of celebrating the Sundays in order, designated by ordinal numbers: first, second, third, and so on. Lectionary-based resources for the Christian year make use of this pattern by cataloguing suggested prayers and songs according to their "proper" numbers—as in Proper 4, Proper 17, or Proper 28. Each of these refers to a specific and consistent set of lectionary readings and the liturgical texts associated with those Scriptures. The names "Nth Sunday in Ordinary Time" or "Nth Sunday after Pentecost" can be harder to pin down because of the changing date of Easter.

Rather than listing "27th Sunday in Ordinary Time" at the beginning of a printed or projected order of worship, consider simply using the date: "Sunday, October 2." The former might give the impression we are perpetuating an obscure and archaic chronology, or wearily marking time as with scratches on a prison wall. The latter suggests that we are ready to meet the breaking news of the day with the good news of the gospel.

Sundays in ordinary time are what we make of them—or better yet, what God makes of them. When we greet them with the energy, intelligence, imagination, and love of an average third-grader, God may use them to reorder our lives.

53 Do Presbyterians believe in saints?

The biblical writers seemed to believe in saints. The Old Testament includes numerous references to the *hasid* (translated as the "loyal," "godly," "faithful," or "saints") and the *tzaddiq* (translated as the "righteous," "just," or "upright"); similarly, the New Testament makes multiple mentions of the *hagios* (translated as the "holy," "righteous," or "saints"). When we consider these verses in their larger scriptural context, they don't seem to refer to perfect paragons of piety but to the ordinary people of God—fallible and flawed yet nevertheless justified and sanctified by God's grace.

Through the history of the church, saints began to take on a different significance as Christians commemorated the lives of particular believers who bore witness to the light of Christ. This began with memorials of the martyrs, whose deaths were celebrated as heavenly birthdays, the completion of their baptism. Sadly, there were soon so many martyrs that it became difficult to remember them all. All Saints' Day, established on November 1 in the ninth century, provided a way to be sure no one was omitted.

Indeed, by the time of the Reformation there were so many saints' days on the church's calendar that they threatened to crowd the primary celebrations of the Christian year. Reformers abolished this cycle of commemorations, arguing that it created false hierarchies and intermediaries (other than Christ), perpetuated the doctrine of salvation through good works, and distracted from the worship of God alone. But they didn't deny the existence of the communion of saints—the great cloud of witnesses surrounding us (Heb. 12:1), the faithful of every time and place.

Thanks to our gradual recovery of the liturgical year and renewed appreciation for the wisdom of the ecumenical church, it is now not uncommon for Presbyterians to commemorate All Saints' Day. We observe this day, however, with an emphasis on the sanctification of the whole people of God in the sense that is described in the biblical examples above. We may also take advantage of All Saints' Day as an opportunity to give thanks for particular figures who have instructed or challenged us, to remember those in our community who have died in the past year, and to pray that we may one day be counted among that great number.

Some Reformed Christians have even begun to reconsider the value of a calendar of commemorations—not as a cycle of saints to be worshiped but as a way to remember and learn from our history, seek insight and inspiration for the present, and find hope and vision for the future. We don't pray *to* the saints, but we may certainly pray *with* them. Through the mystery of our baptism, we have been united with them in the body of Christ. We sing with them, even now, as they worship around God's throne.

After all, we believe in resurrection. And if we believe in resurrection, there is a sense in which the dead are not really dead to us. This is why we say, in the words of the Apostles' Creed, "I believe in the Holy Spirit, the holy catholic church, the communion of saints, the forgiveness of sins, the resurrection of the body, and the life everlasting. Amen."

54 What about Mother's Day and the Fourth of July?

As the name suggests, the Christian year is centered around none other than Jesus Christ. The festivals of the liturgical calendar are primarily rooted in the story of salvation—specifically, Christ's incarnation, life, death, resurrection, and promised return. This is why so many of these days have the title "of the Lord," as in Baptism of the Lord or Transfiguration of the Lord. A handful of other special days are rooted in different biblical images and events (Ash Wednesday, Day of Pentecost) or theological affirmations (Trinity Sunday, Christ the King Sunday). But at the center remains this great mystery of faith: Christ has died; Christ is risen; Christ will come again.

There are countless other events on our calendars—cultural observances, historical commemorations, civic holidays, community festivals, significant anniversaries, and programmatic emphases of the church. In the celebration of the Christian year, these events—as important as they may be—take second place to the proclamation of God's saving work in Jesus Christ. We don't have special orders of worship for these days as we do for the events of Jesus' life, death, and resurrection in Holy Week. There aren't lectionary readings for these occasions since they aren't rooted in particular stories of Scripture.

But this doesn't mean we can or should ignore these days in worship. Christian worship is always in dialogue with the events and concerns of our culture, even when it challenges or critiques them. We can and should acknowledge these other days on the calendar—through announcements, preaching, prayers, and other activities of the church.

The liturgical calendar is organized around the life, death, resurrection, and promised return of Christ. And Jesus Christ is the one who—even from the cross—reaches out to embrace the whole world God loves so much. In Christ we meet the God who cares for us as a mother hen shelters her young. In Christ we meet the God who sets us free from sin and death forever. In this way, the gospel speaks to the celebrations and concerns of our culture through the seasons and festivals of the Christian year.

7

Special Services

55 What is daily prayer?

"It is good to give thanks to the LORD, to sing praises to your name, O Most High; to declare your steadfast love in the morning, and your faithfulness by night" (Ps. 92:1–2). Like so many of the psalms, Psalm 92 describes the ancient practice of turning to God in prayer and praise throughout the hours of the day. In the early church, patterns of Jewish worship from the temple and synagogue were adopted and adapted to fit the needs of the first Christians. Monastic communities, devoted to a common life of worship and service, further developed the discipline of the daily office as they shaped specific forms of prayer for particular times of the day and night. These patterns of prayer have been passed down through generations of disciples and are now widespread throughout the ecumenical church and around the globe.

Contemporary Presbyterian resources, such as the 2018 *Book of Common Worship*, offer a fourfold pattern for daily prayer: evening, night, morning, and midday. The primary services are evening and morning—at the "hinges" of the day, those twilight transitions between light and darkness, work and rest, waking and sleep. The evening and morning services may be slightly longer and more elaborate, since these are the most likely to be practiced in the company of others—at a small group meeting, a church retreat, or family gathering, for instance. Conversely, the services for prayer at night and midday are shorter and simpler, as these tend to be used just before sleeping or in the midst of a busy day, respectively.

The beauty of daily prayer is that it is so simple—a spiritual discipline that can be practiced by anyone, with any number of people, in any setting, and in a short span of time. The basic ingredients are psalms, Scripture, and prayer, framed by biblical words of greeting and blessing. Other elements that may be included are canticles, additional psalms or hymns, devotional or confessional readings, a thanksgiving for light (at evening prayer), a prayer of confession (at night prayer), and a thanksgiving for baptism (at morning prayer). The pattern of daily prayer is easily learned and can be used even when Bibles and prayer books are not available. A note card with a psalm verse, portion of the weekly lectionary, and list of prayer concerns can become a portable resource for daily prayer.

For Christians, the rhythm of daily prayer is a way of living out our baptism—a daily practice of dying and rising with Christ. Daily prayer helps us learn to rest in Christ's peace each evening and rise each day to walk in newness of life. As with the seasons and festivals of the Christian year and the weekly celebration of resurrection on the Lord's Day, daily prayer is a way to keep time with Christ and inhabit the mystery of our faith.

The practice of daily prayer is intended to be a gift of time in communion with God, not a chore or obligation. Just as the moon, stars, and sun proceed in their courses without any human intervention, the worship of God goes on all around us, before and after us, within us and without us. Daily prayer is an invitation to join in this cosmic dance of the church with the whole creation.

56 What is confirmation?

Our contemporary traditions around confirmation are the result of centuries of development and a variety of theological, pastoral, and practical considerations in the history of the church.

Among the earliest Christians, people first heard the Word proclaimed, were inspired to prepare for and receive baptism, and then immediately shared in the Lord's Supper. When Christianity became the established religion of the Roman Empire in the early fourth century, the process of Christian initiation grew longer and more elaborate, including anointing by a bishop before Communion—the origin of what we now call confirmation.

In subsequent centuries, however, high rates of infant mortality and the doctrine of original sin prompted people to baptize children as soon as possible. Bishops weren't able to keep up with the demand for baptisms, so among Western churches the rite of anointing that preceded Communion was put off until a later date. Gradually, through the Middle Ages, baptism, confirmation, and (first) Communion became three separate liturgical acts.

This continued to be the case among Reformed churches as well, although John Calvin and other Reformers sought to restore and preserve the unity of Word and sacraments through an emphasis on covenant theology and the use of catechisms in faith formation. In the 1970s, Presbyterian churches changed their polity to receive baptized children at the Lord's Supper without waiting for confirmation; yet the practice of confirmation—as reaffirmation of baptism upon profession of faith—has remained an important rite of passage for young people in the church, a chance to claim for themselves the promises of their baptism.

The liturgy for confirmation (also called "Profession of Faith" in the 2018 *Book of Common Worship*) looks very similar to that of baptism. It takes place around the font and includes the following: a presentation from a member of the church's session; a profession of faith in which candidates renounce evil, turn to Jesus Christ, and affirm their faith with the whole congregation using the words of the Apostles' Creed; a prayer over the water for the reaffirmation of baptism; the laying on of hands and anointing with oil; and the sharing of signs of peace as a welcome into active participation and full responsibility in the governance and mission of the church. The only element of the baptismal liturgy that is missing, of course, is baptism with water in the name of the triune God, since those who are to be confirmed are already baptized. On occasions when certain members of the church's confirmation class have not yet been baptized, the *Book of Common Worship* provides an order of worship for combined baptism and confirmation.

57 What happens at an ordination?

Like the order of worship for confirmation, the service of ordination contains many echoes of the baptismal liturgy. This is fitting,
as the sacrament of baptism is each Christian's "primary ordination" into the universal ministry of the church. Through the gift
and calling of our baptism, God claims all of us as "a royal priesthood" (1 Pet. 2:9), empowered by the Holy Spirit and dedicated to
Christ's service. Every one of us has a Christian vocation; in this
sense, each of us is a minister in Christ's church.

Ordination builds on this idea of the "priesthood of all believers" by giving us a way to acknowledge God's particular gift and
calling to particular people—those who are ordained as deacons,
ruling elders, and ministers of Word and Sacrament. These are the
three "ordered ministries" (formerly called "offices") recognized
in the Presbyterian Church (U.S.A.). Persons who are called to
these ministries are not extra-baptized or more Christian than other
members of the church. Rather, they are anointed for humble service in the name of the one who knelt to wash his disciples' feet
and served them at table. Furthermore, we believe that they are
called to carry out this service in collegial and collaborative ways,
always subject to the authority of Christ as expressed through the
Scriptures and the discernment of the church. Ordered ministry is
a gift of God to the church, as those who are ordained are entrusted
to lead in Christ's work of compassion, witness, and service (deacons), discernment and governance (ruling elders), and the proclamation of the gospel and celebration of the sacraments (pastors).

As noted above, the liturgy for ordination typically takes place
around the font and includes many features in common with the
baptismal service. The distinctive element of ordination, as recognized throughout the ecumenical church, is the laying on of hands
with prayer for the Holy Spirit. This act, based on biblical models
of ordination, emphasizes the continuity of ministry and teaching
among the people of God throughout the ages and expresses our
utter reliance on the work of the Spirit in acts of Christian service. In the PC(USA), another distinctive aspect of the ordination

liturgy is a set of "Constitutional Questions" from the *Book of Order*. Anointing with oil—an ancient and biblical sign of ordination—may also be included as a tangible reaffirmation of baptism and sign of the gifts of the Spirit.

When people who have already been ordained are installed to a new term of service, whether on the board of deacons or elders or as pastor in a new congregation, a similar service is held. The difference is that the laying on of hands is not repeated for those who are already ordained.

Baptism has been called the "sacrament of equality," for in Christ distinctions of race, status, and gender are dissolved (see Gal. 3:27–28). Presbyterians believe that anyone who is baptized can also be ordained to any ministry in the church. This means that women and men are eligible for any form of service and leadership. It is not the same as saying every person has the "right" to be ordained, however, as ordination only comes after a process of careful and prayerful discernment through the councils of the church.

In Presbyterian theology and practice, the liturgy for ordination is essentially the same whether one is ordained as a deacon, ruling elder, or pastor. There are only minor differences in the order of worship for these occasions, related to the specific gifts and callings of these ordered ministries. This too is fitting, as the service for ordination is really about *one* call to ministry—that of Jesus Christ, extended to all.

58 What is a service of wholeness?

One of the main things we know about Jesus from the Gospels is that he was—and is—a healer. Stories of Jesus' healing work abound—he restores sight to people who are blind, hearing and speech to those who are deaf, and mobility to those who are paralyzed; he casts out evil spirits, cures people with leprosy, and even raises the dead; he gives life, comfort, and peace to countless others around Galilee, Samaria, and Judea. Given the prevalence of such events in the accounts of Jesus' life, it is somewhat surprising that so many mainline churches have not taken up this aspect of his ministry.

Then again, perhaps it isn't so surprising. We have come to put a lot of trust in medical science, diagnostic technology, surgical intervention, pharmaceutical treatment, psychiatric therapy, nutritional guidelines, and preventative care. We visit doctors for ailments of the flesh and pastors for afflictions of the spirit. We are willing and eager to pray for those who are sick, but we don't want to raise false hopes or make promises on which we cannot hope to deliver. Most of all, we are reticent to be associated with television faith healers who make extravagant claims about their miraculous powers—and often make a lot of money in the process.

In the Presbyterian/Reformed tradition, a service of wholeness makes it clear that healing—if and when it comes—always and only comes as a gracious gift from God. We may serve as instruments of God's healing, but such power is ultimately beyond our comprehension or control. We have faith that God can provide for us in our distress, but we also understand that full and abundant life may not come in a way we desire, expect, or imagine. Healing—in the most holistic sense of body, mind, heart, and soul—may not be the same thing as convalescence, cure, recovery, or remission. This is part of the reason such liturgies are known as services of "healing and wholeness"—a name that suggests a broader sense of God's *shalom*.

A service of healing and wholeness is, at essence, a service of prayer—prayer that may be accompanied and enacted with the laying on of hands and/or anointing with oil (actions that are carefully interpreted in light of the observations above). A service of healing and wholeness should include the reading of Scripture and the proclamation of God's Word as the source of our life and peace. The reaffirmation of baptism or celebration of the Lord's Supper may also be offered as a sign and seal of the transforming grace of God.

Services of healing and wholeness may be organized on a quarterly or monthly basis in a community or congregation, or they may be included as a regular component of the service for the Lord's Day. They may be adapted for use in homes, hospitals, or hospice care, provided that these occasions are presented as the work of the larger church and not an individual minister. Such services thus provide a way for the church to carry out its pastoral care in the context of worship—and to continue the healing ministry of the Lord Jesus Christ.

59 What does a wedding have to do with worship?

Around the world, throughout history, and in various faiths and cultures, weddings serve a number of important social functions—establishing family bonds, legitimizing sexual relationships, and providing a context for the nurture of children. In the context of Christian community, a marriage ceremony may do all of these things. But as a service of worship, it also testifies to the great faithfulness of God, the self-giving love of Jesus Christ, and the reconciling work of the Holy Spirit. A service of marriage may even give us a glimpse of the life of the world to come—the marriage supper of the Lamb, when heaven and earth become one.

The order of worship for a stand-alone service of marriage may have a similar shape to the Service for the Lord's Day—gathering, Word, Eucharist, and sending—with the rite of marriage taking place between the Word and the Eucharist. In fact, a marriage service may take place within the context of Sunday worship. More commonly, however, services of marriage occur at a special time and/or place set apart for this purpose. In these situations, the liturgy may be abridged or adapted to account for the setting of the service and the nature of the gathered community.

A service of marriage typically begins with a procession—entrance of those who are to wed, sometimes accompanied by family members and friends. After opening words and a prayer by the presider, the couple declare their desire and intent to be married; this may take place at the baptismal font. Those in attendance are asked to affirm their support for the couple: first the families and then the whole congregation. Passages of Scripture are read, and a brief sermon follows.

The primary action of marriage takes place with the exchange of vows; these words may also be spoken at the font, as they rely on the grace of God poured out in the covenant of baptism. Joining hands, the couple promise to be loving and faithful partners throughout all the seasons of their life together. Identical vows express equality and mutuality between those who are joined in marriage. The couple may also exchange rings or other symbols of their love; the circle of the wedding ring symbolizes unity and eternity. The presider prays for the couple in their new life together and then announces their marriage. A kiss of peace may be shared between the couple, and signs of peace may be exchanged among all who are gathered.

If the Lord's Supper is celebrated, it follows the sharing of Christ's peace. The service of marriage ends with a charge to the couple and a blessing for the whole assembly.

It is all too easy for a service of marriage to lose its focus on the worship of God. The couple can be consumed with decisions about music, flowers, apparel, attendants, invitations—not to mention wedding showers, gift registries, rehearsal dinners, reception banquets, and honeymoon voyages. Those who plan and lead the marriage service must be careful not to lose sight of the primary purpose of this and every liturgical event—to glorify God.

Marriage is a momentous decision, a serious commitment, and a challenging new vocation. For Christians called to enter into this way of life together, it becomes a context for sharing the grace of Jesus Christ, the love of God, and the communion of the Holy Spirit. By the grace of God, it can even be a sign of the life of the world to come.

60 Why is the funeral called a service of witness to the resurrection?

"We do not want you to be uninformed," Paul wrote to the Thessalonians, "about those who have died, so that you may not grieve as others do who have no hope. For since we believe that Jesus died and rose again, even so, through Jesus, God will bring with him those who have died" (1 Thess. 4:13–14). Our hope in the promise of the risen Lord is critical in understanding the shape and significance of the Christian funeral, a service of witness to the resurrection.

The funeral service begins with a greeting in the name of the Lord Jesus Christ, who shared our death so that he might destroy death's power and lead us to everlasting life. A thanksgiving for baptism may follow. As those who have participated in Jesus' dying and rising through the sacrament of baptism, we rejoice—for the one who has died, baptism is now complete; she or he will now share in the risen life of Christ forever. Sentences of Scripture, opening prayers, hymns of the church, and the confession and pardon complete the gathering part of the funeral service.

The funeral continues with reading and proclamation from Scripture—a message of hope in God's victory over the powers of sin and death through Jesus Christ. This part of the order of worship may also include an affirmation of faith, more congregational singing, and brief expressions of gratitude for the one who has died; it concludes with prayers of thanksgiving, intercession, and supplication. Through all of these actions, we offer an account of the hope that is in us (1 Pet. 3:15). We bear witness to our conviction that death will not have the last word.

Including the Eucharist in the funeral service is another compelling way to bear witness to the transforming power of Christ's resurrection. After all, it was in the breaking of the bread on the road to Emmaus that the disciples finally recognized their risen Lord (Luke 24:31). Around the Lord's Table we remember and proclaim the mystery of our faith and join with the company of the faithful in every time and place in celebrating God's saving love.

The sending is the most distinctive movement of the funeral service. It may take place in the church before the burial or after a procession to the graveside. Wherever it occurs, this part of the order of worship begins with the commendation of the one who has died to the Lord. A sentence from the liturgy here beautifully encapsulates the spirit of this service of witness to the resurrection: "All of us go down to the dust; yet even at the grave we make our song: Alleluia, alleluia, alleluia" (*Book of Common Worship*,

793). The presider offers God's blessing to the congregation. And then all sing or say the Song of Simeon or *Nunc Dimittis* (Luke 2:29–32): "Now, Lord, you let your servant go in peace: your word has been fulfilled" (*Book of Common Worship*, 794).

The committal is an extension of the sending, in which the one who has died is committed to the earth. This may take place at the graveside, crematorium, or columbarium; at sea; or at the location where the ashes are dispersed. (In cases where the committal of the body takes place before the church's worship, the liturgy is adapted accordingly, and the event is called a memorial service.) Like every aspect of the funeral service, the committal is steeped in Scripture that proclaims the hope and promise of the gospel: "'I am the resurrection and the life,'" says the Lord (John 11:25).

"Therefore encourage one another with these words," Paul concluded (1 Thess. 4:18). At a service of witness to the resurrection, this is precisely what we do. Even in the shadow of the valley of death, we testify to the good news of Jesus Christ.

61 Should the casket be open or closed?

Like many events in Christian worship, the funeral presents us with a paradox. Out of the depths of our grief we bear witness to the good news of the resurrection. Faced with the finality of death we proclaim the promise of everlasting life. With tears in our eyes, we sing alleluias.

The question of whether the casket should be open or closed illustrates this theological tension within the Christian funeral. Having the casket open can compel us to grapple with the reality of death and to begin to do the necessary pastoral work of mourning. We are forced to let go of the illusions and euphemisms we use to shield ourselves from death's full impact. Having the casket closed can allow us to proclaim Christ's victory over death and to begin to imagine the wonder of everlasting life in God's new creation. We are able to wonder with the apostle, "'Where, O death, is your victory? Where, O death, is your sting?'" (1 Cor. 15:55).

Fortunately, we are not forced to choose between these options.

The casket may remain open during the visitation or viewing before the funeral in order that family and friends may pay their final respects to the deceased. But it should be closed by the time the service begins so that the funeral may truly be a service of witness to the resurrection. The placing of the pall—a white cloth symbolic of being clothed with Christ's righteousness in baptism—marks this turn at the beginning of the funeral liturgy. Water may be sprinkled on the casket at this time.

Of course, there are situations in which it is not possible or appropriate to open the casket or when people choose to be cremated. In these cases, the presence of the casket or urn suffices as a visual sign of the reality of death among us. There are also times when the one who has died is buried before the church gathers for a memorial service. In these cases, the words of the presider bear more of the weight of the pastoral work at hand.

This is the essential paradox of Christian faith—that in the death of Jesus Christ our Savior, we come to know and share the promise of abundant and eternal life. Even as earthly life comes to a close, the Christian funeral helps us to remain open to this good news.

8

Music and Art in Worship

62 Why do we sing in worship?

Bible scholars believe that one of the oldest fragments of Scripture is actually a song—Miriam's song, to be specific, in Exodus 15:21: "'Sing to the LORD, for [God] has triumphed gloriously.'" While other passages speak of previous persons and earlier events, the archaic style of the Hebrew in this "Song of the Sea" suggests that it is one of the most ancient texts in the biblical canon. From the beginning, the people of God have raised their voices in song to praise God for our salvation. Why is singing so important?

Singing helps to define sacred space and time. Something powerful and profound happens when we sing together in worship. It is immediately clear to all—whether they are in the sanctuary or listening in from the street—that this is a different kind of event. When there is singing, it is impossible to mistake worship for a town hall meeting, academic lecture, or business conference. Something holy is happening.

Singing transcends mere speech. Music communicates something that words alone cannot convey. Speaking alone does not do justice to the good news of God's saving love. Perhaps this is why the psalmists keep exclaiming, "Sing a new song!" and why people like Moses, Miriam, Hannah, Zechariah, Mary, and Simeon keep breaking into song throughout the pages of the Bible.

Singing builds community. Our minds are united around the words, images, and themes of a common text. Our spirits get in tune with one another through a common melody or harmony. Our bodies dance, clap, sway, and breathe together to the pulse of a common meter, rhythm, and tempo. Recent research suggests that singing together may even synchronize our heartbeats. What better image of the body of Christ?

Singing stays with us. As we go forth from worship, the melodies, rhythms, and harmonies of sacred songs accompany us in our daily lives. They help us to tune our stories to God's story. They enable us to order our steps according to God's word. They inspire us to seek harmony through reconciliation in our relationships and peace in the world.

63 What is a hymn?

A classic definition of *hymn* comes from the commentary of the great theologian Augustine on Psalm 148:

> Do you know what a hymn is? It is singing to the praise of God. If you praise God and do not sing, you utter no hymn. If you praise anything which does not pertain to the praise of God— though in singing you praise, you utter no hymn. A hymn then contains these three things: song, and praise, and that of God. (*Expositions of the Psalms*, Ps. 148.11)

Augustine gives us a very good place to start: a hymn is the praise of God in song.

But this definition doesn't quite reflect the diversity of the church's song as it has developed from the earliest centuries of the church to the present day. The New Testament epistles themselves include two references to "psalms, hymns, and spiritual songs" (Eph. 5:19; Col. 3:16), indicating that Christian song took a variety of forms, even at the very beginning.

In common, contemporary use, a "hymn" in Presbyterian worship might be one of many things—a Genevan psalm setting, a Guarani *Kyrie*, a Gregorian chant, a Gaelic folk tune, a Gloria Patri, a German chorale, a Ghanaian doxology, and so on. It might address God directly (in the second person), extol God's mighty acts (in the third person), or even reflect God's own words in Scripture (in the first person). The primary theme might well be praise or thanksgiving, but depending on the circumstances it might be petition, confession, or lament instead.

A hymn can be a time machine, transporting us to another era of church history, or a passport, allowing us to sing with Christians in a distant land. A hymn can be an out-of-body experience, lifting our hearts and spirits on high, or an in-the-body experience, moving our hands and feet to the rhythm of God at work. A hymn can be a three-minute theology course, informing our exegesis, ecclesiology, or eschatology. It can be a picket sign, demonstrating our resistance against oppressive powers, or a family heirloom, marked with the faith and faithfulness of generations. A hymn can be a private diary page, giving us a glimpse of the insights and struggles of the saints.

Think of hymns and other congregational songs as something like incense. They fill the air of the church at worship, making the place thick with meaning and mystery. They are a sign of our offering of thanks and praise and a symbol of the prayers we lift to the Lord. Even as the scent of incense goes with worshipers into the world, the church's song remains on our lips and in our hearts.

It is important for us to remember that every beloved old hymn was once a strange new song. Even as we treasure our favorite hymns of faith, we must make room for the new songs we are called to sing, as worshipers have done in every generation.

64 Why do Presbyterians sing psalms?

In the Protestant Reformation, church leaders sought to rebuild Christian worship from the ground up. They wanted to get back to basics, adhering to scriptural models for worship and using biblical texts as much as possible. This impulse led some of our theological ancestors to commend the psalms (and other biblical songs) as the only appropriate songs for use in Christian worship. "Why don't we sing the songs God gave us to sing," they asked, "the songs that God's people have been singing for millennia?"

Although Presbyterians and other Reformed Christians have expanded our musical repertoire over the past five hundred years, we still have a strong tradition of singing the psalms, especially in metrical settings (hymnlike paraphrases of the biblical psalms). There are many good reasons for continuing this tradition into the twenty-first century and beyond.

As our Reformed forebears observed, the psalms connect us with the worship of the people of God through the ages. They are living history—at least as long as we continue to sing them—joining our voices with the songs of the faithful in every generation. This is a remarkable musical, cultural, and liturgical heritage. What else can we say we've been doing for three thousand years?

The psalms also teach us to pray. They provide language and grammar for prayer in times of peril and praise, despair and delight, worry and wonder. They broaden the horizons of our prayer, challenging us to turn to God in every situation, showing us that there is nothing we cannot offer to the Lord. Whatever you're going through, there's a psalm for it.

There are many ways to sing the psalms. While Reformed churches have historically specialized in hymnic settings of the psalms, modern church music gives us a great array of options: praise choruses, global songs, contemplative chants, poetic paraphrases, cantillated recitation, responsorial refrains, and more. Part of the incredible gift of this ancient body of song is that it continues to inspire so many contemporary and diverse musical expressions.

65 Do we need to have a choir?

There already is a choir. The question is whether we want to join it. Isaiah heard a choir of seraphs chanting, "'Holy, holy, holy'" in God's temple (Isa. 6:1–8). Out of the whirlwind, the Lord reveals to Job how the morning stars sang together at the dawn of creation (Job 38:7). When Jesus was born, a multitude of the heavenly host sang, "'Glory to God in the highest'" (Luke 2:13–14). When he entered Jerusalem, the crowds called out, "'Blessed is the king,'" and Jesus said, "'If these were silent, the stones would shout out'" (Luke 19:37–40). Around God's heavenly throne, the living creatures and elders join in the chorus: "'You are worthy, our Lord and God'" (Rev. 4:11).

The church's primary choir is the congregation itself. In the Christian understanding of ministry, all of the baptized are called "to be a holy priesthood, to offer spiritual sacrifices acceptable to God through Jesus Christ" (1 Pet. 2:5). Joining the great song of the seraphs and saints—and yes, even the stars and stones—is an important part of the ministry of all the faithful, the priesthood of all believers. It doesn't matter whether you can carry a tune or have a trained voice. We are all being carried along by the heavenly host and trained for a part in the celestial choir.

When a church has a special choir—rehearsed and/or robed— their primary role is to support the congregation in singing. These singers can be very helpful in introducing new material, under-girding challenging passages, and encouraging the people of God to lift their voices with confidence. They may also offer anthems, introits, and other special selections to enhance the church's prayer and praise, but such offerings are never to replace or compete with the congregation's song.

If the book of Revelation is any indication, there will be plenty of singing in the life that is to come. Why not get started now so that we will be ready to join the great multitude and chorus of angels, singing,

> "Amen! Blessing and glory and wisdom
> and thanksgiving and honor
> and power and might
> be to our God forever and ever!
>   Amen."
>   (Rev. 7:12)

66 What is the purpose of instrumental music?

The purpose of everything that happens in worship is to help us glorify and enjoy God. Instrumental music—whether it comes from an organ, a piano, an electric guitar, a brass ensemble, a drum circle, or a handbell choir—should serve this same "chief end." An instrumental musical selection should be an offering of reverence and devotion to God, drawing worshipers into the spirit of praise and prayer.

Because such offerings do not include words, however, it can be more difficult for worshipers to understand their intent and prayerfully participate in them as acts of worship. Without thoughtful integration into the church's liturgy, instrumental music can feel like a brief performance or recital, sandwiched into the service of worship. Here are some suggestions for helping instrumental musical offerings to connect with the congregation, and vice versa.

Carefully consider the shape and flow of the order of worship and how instrumental music might contribute to (or detract from) the action of the liturgy at any given moment. Music at the gathering should help to prepare worshipers for an encounter with God. Music during the offering should inspire them to devote themselves to Christ's service. Music during Communion should draw them to the joyful feast of the risen Lord. Music at the sending should propel them out into the world to share in the Spirit's work. (All the same considerations apply for choral anthems.)

Where a printed or projected order of worship is used, one might offer some relevant information about the instrumental musical selection. It can be as simple as translating a title in a foreign language, or if the piece is based on a hymn tune, one might indicate the familiar title of the hymn and its number in the hymnal. If appropriate, a brief description of the piece and its connection to the worship service may be included, or guidance on how to pray at this time can be given.

Avoid the temptation to use instrumental music as filler for silence. Intentional, prayerful silence has its own place in a service of worship and can speak in a way that is every bit as powerful as song. Use music prayerfully and deliberately for the glory of God, and allow times of silence to reverberate with the awe and wonder of the Holy One.

67 What is the purpose of visual art?

Christians in the Reformed tradition have had an uneasy relationship with visual art. We have inherited a healthy concern about the danger of idolatry, but we have also begun to appreciate the variety of ways in which God's beauty, truth, and goodness are revealed.

At the time of the Reformation, liturgy in the Western church was conducted in Latin. For most worshipers, therefore, the liturgy was not so much a verbal experience as a visual event. Stained-glass windows, statues, and other iconography had to bear much of the weight of telling the story of salvation, conveying the mystery of faith, and declaring the glory of God. People typically only received Communion once a year, so the Mass became a spectator event—watching the priest celebrate the sacrament. This was a rather limited form of participation.

In contrast, the Protestant Reformers brought a strong emphasis on faith as something that comes through the hearing of the Word (Rom. 10:17). Accordingly, they translated the Bible and the liturgy into the common languages of the people of God, transforming worship from a visual experience to an auditory event. This was an important course correction, but in retrospect we can see that they may have overemphasized the intellectual dimension of faith, expressed through the written and spoken word.

The Reformers also brought a deep concern about the danger of idolatry. John Calvin, for instance, famously referred to the human heart as a "perpetual factory of idols" (*Institutes*, 1.11.8). This concern was related, in part, to the proliferation of saints' days and other popular devotions that had come to detract from the worship of God alone. Consequently, many of the Reformers stripped their churches of visual imagery in order that these symbols not compete with the proclamation of the saving Word of God.

In our time, Presbyterian/Reformed Christians are beginning to have a greater appreciation for the aesthetic qualities of worship. We remain vigilant about the peril of idolatry, but we also understand that visual art can contribute to the same purpose as the spoken word—to teach the story of salvation, proclaim the good news of Jesus Christ, and convey the glory of God. Our eyes are opened to the new things God is doing. We are ready to "come and see" (Ps. 66:5; John 1:39) the mighty works of the Lord.

68 What is the difference between art and idolatry?

There is a sixteenth-century painting of the crucifixion by Matthias Grünewald known as the Isenheim Altarpiece. At the center of the image is Jesus on the cross—but in the foreground we see John the Baptist, holding the Scriptures in one hand and, with the other, pointing an enormous finger at the suffering Savior. The twentieth-century theologian Karl Barth famously kept a reproduction of this picture over his desk. For Barth, John's posture in this painting was an apt depiction of the theologian's task: to point to Christ.

This is also the role of art in Christian worship: pointing to God and to what God has done, is doing, and will do in Jesus Christ and by the power of the Holy Spirit. Human expressions of creativity in worship—whether visual, musical, dramatic, poetic, kinesthetic, or otherwise—should always direct attention to the goodness, grace, and glory of our divine Creator. When they do so, they glorify God and edify the church. When they do not, they can be a dangerous stumbling block in Christian worship.

The Ten Commandments include a strong prohibition against the creation of false idols or graven images. The problem with such figures, as so vividly demonstrated in the story of Aaron and the golden calf (see Exod. 32), is when we give them the adoration and acclaim due to God alone. There is only one who has the power to redeem us; there is only one who is worthy of our worship. "The LORD is our God, the LORD alone" (Deut. 6:4).

When we talk about the danger of idolatry in modern worship, however, we are not just talking about golden calves. It might be a sermon illustration, a set of candles, a prayer book, a projection screen, an organ prelude, a guitar solo, a floral arrangement, a choral anthem, or a charismatic leader. All of these things can be used for the glory of God, but all of them are also susceptible to unhealthy attachment, misplaced adulation, and vain applause.

Of course, such determinations are highly subjective. This question, then, is one that requires prayerful reflection and constant vigilance for planners and leaders of worship. It calls us to seek the wisdom of God, the mind of Christ, and the discernment of the Holy Spirit. Perhaps the best touchstone is that image of John the Baptist, pointing to Christ. As John said, "'He must increase, and I must decrease'" (John 3:30). Any artistic offering in worship must seek to magnify the Lord our God, the Lord alone.

9

Worship Space

69 Does it matter where we worship?

At a certain level, no—it doesn't matter where we worship. We worship the Maker of heaven and earth. Jesus taught on hillsides and in synagogues; he broke bread in houses and by the sea. As the wind blows where it chooses, the Spirit of God cannot be contained. Thus, for Christians, there is no sacred mountain or holy city that is more appropriate for worship than any other. There is no place—however sacred or profane, however grand or humble— that cannot be transformed into hallowed ground by the presence of God.

The psalmists seemed to understand this especially well. The earth and everything in it belong to God (Ps. 24:1). There is no place where we can escape God's presence (Ps. 139:7). The word of God goes out to the ends of the earth (Ps. 19:4).

Nevertheless, we must also remember that places of worship for the people of God have a profound impact on our formation as disciples. They may shape our understanding of the divine, as a Gothic stone cathedral resonates with the greatness and glory of God. They may cultivate our piety, as a wood-frame country church stands at the edge of a furrowed field. They may provide the parameters in which we practice our faith, as a suburban sanctuary sets apart a space for worship. They may challenge us to witness and service, as a coffee-house congregation meets amid the clamor of daily life.

A space for Christian worship must provide for the proclamation of the Word and the celebration of the sacraments (more about that in subsequent questions). These basic marks of our liturgical life are how we identify the presence and action of the risen Lord among us.

As our Directory for Worship maintains, a space for Christian worship must also "encourage community, be accessible to all, and open us to reverence for God" (*Book of Order*, W-1.0203). Each of these dimensions of liturgical space is worth exploring.

Do our places of worship draw us closer to one another as we draw close to God? A space for Christian worship should help us to experience our connection in the body of Christ. It should promote deeper relationship—among the community of faith and within the communion of the triune God. Ample gathering space, the arrangement of seating, and the physical relationship between leaders and people are among the important factors to consider.

Do our places of worship promote the full participation of the whole body of Christ? A space for Christian worship should provide for the active engagement of people of various ages and abilities. It should clearly demonstrate that opportunities for leadership and service are open to all. The accessibility and flexibility of the chancel, sanctuary, fellowship hall, educational space, and other parts of the church facility speak volumes in this regard.

Do our places of worship inspire us to give blessing and honor and glory to God? A space for Christian worship should evoke our gratitude for God's amazing grace. It should provoke us to offer our lives in Christ's service. Art, architecture, and other elements of the liturgical environment help to awaken our theological imaginations and move us to respond to God's call.

70 What are the parts of the worship space?

In any place for Christian worship, the most important visual image or "symbol" on display is not a liturgical furnishing or stained-glass window but the gathering of the people of God—an icon of the body of Christ, a microcosm of the universal church, a subcommittee of the communion of saints. Accordingly, the central and primary part of our worship space is the nave. This word, derived from the Latin word for ship (as in navy), reflects the classic metaphor of the church as a ship (think of Noah's ark or Jesus crossing the Sea of Galilee) as well as the fact that the vaulted ceilings of many great cathedrals resemble the inverted hull of a boat. The congregational space may also be called the sanctuary, a word that means holy place but also carries the connotation of a safe place or shelter. The word *sanctuary* is often used to refer to the whole place of worship, but in a technical sense, it refers especially to this space for the gathering of the congregation. The nave or sanctuary may include fixed seating or movable chairs. Ideally, it is a space that is flexible enough to accommodate different numbers of people, allow for a variety of liturgical events, and offer ample room for movement.

A place for Christian worship must include spaces for the proclamation of the Word and celebration of the sacraments—the distinguishing marks or "notes" of the church. Typically, these actions take place in or around the chancel, an area for worship leadership. Preaching takes place at the pulpit; if there is a second (often smaller) reading stand, it is called the lectern. The table for the Lord's Supper may be elevated on the chancel or at floor level in the front of the sanctuary. Similarly, the baptismal font may be on the chancel, in the front of the sanctuary, or even at the doors of the church; if the font is in the back of the sanctuary, there must be sufficient space for gathering around the font and seating that allows for the congregation to turn and face the font as needed. The presider and other worship leaders may remain in the chancel throughout the service or may come forward from the congregation.

A worship space may include a special place for the choir. It may be part of the chancel, in a transept (an arm or wing of the sanctuary), or in an elevated loft in the back or front of the room. In some churches, the choir sits among the congregation and gathers in a designated place only when it is time to sing.

An important part of the worship space we often forget is the doors of the church. The doors connect the church with the world around us. They facilitate the dynamic movements of gathering and sending that frame the service of worship. As such, they symbolize the church's identity and mission—gathering in the name of the triune God and going forth to love and serve God and neighbor.

71 Where should the baptismal font be?

On the premises—that's a start. Unfortunately, some churches don't have a baptismal font in view and only bring it out as needed for the sacrament. "It's been so long since we had a baptism," a pastor may remark, "and we don't have people asking to be baptized anyway." Perhaps the visible presence of a font might help that situation.

Baptism is an essential mark of Christian identity—a sign of Jesus' death and resurrection, the forgiveness of sin, the gifts of the Holy Spirit, incorporation into the body of Christ, and the promise of God's coming realm. In baptism we are inscribed with the name of the triune God, enlisted in the service of Christ, and imprinted with the seal of the Spirit. But the fact that baptism is an invisible mark makes it all too easy to forget these connections to Christian discipleship. The gift of baptism is unclaimed; the calling of baptism is unanswered.

Responding to this problem, the 2006 Presbyterian Church (U.S.A.) sacrament study *Invitation to Christ* called on churches to make baptism more visible—to set the baptismal font in full view of the congregation, open the font and fill it with water on every Lord's Day, and lead appropriate parts of weekly worship from the font and from the table. Churches that have taken up this challenge have begun to rediscover the mystery and meaning of the sacrament and the implications of baptismal discipleship in personal vocation and congregational life.

As noted above, there are various options for the placement of the baptismal font within the sanctuary, each with important symbolic significance. Placing the font near the pulpit emphasizes our understanding of the sacraments as signs of God's promise and seals of God's word. Placing it near the Communion table demonstrates the relationship between baptism (as incorporation into

Christ's body) and the Lord's Supper (as participation in Christ's body). Placing the font in a center aisle of the sanctuary evokes the lifelong journey of baptismal discipleship. Placing it near the doors of the church suggests our entrance into Christ's body and our going forth in Jesus' service.

Wherever the font is placed, its location should allow worshipers to see and sometimes touch the water of the font, provide ample space for gathering (as at baptisms and ordinations), and facilitate leadership from the font (as at the confession and pardon). These simple but important considerations may, by God's grace, inspire newcomers to explore deeper relationship with Christ through baptism and will help all members to remember their baptism with thanksgiving.

Is it a table or an altar?

It is fairly common to see Communion tables inscribed with the words "Do This in Remembrance of Me." Where did Jesus speak these words? At a meal with his disciples—a Passover meal on the night before his death. This inscription makes a strong connection to Jesus' institution of the sacrament (see 1 Cor. 11). It also presents us with a helpful question: What, exactly, is the "this" that Jesus is calling us to do?

Presbyterian/Reformed churches emphasize the idea of the sacrament as a meal with Christ—breaking bread and sharing the cup together in Jesus' name, according to his example. We remember Jesus' institution of the sacrament at the Passover meal (see Luke 22 and parallels), but we also remember other times Jesus broke bread in the Gospels: at the feeding of the multitude (see Luke 9) and after he rose from the dead (see Luke 24). Jesus was famous (even infamous; see Luke 7) for the practices of eating and drinking that characterized his life and ministry. In our tradition, then, the primary meaning of "Do this" is sharing the meal as we gather for the feast that Christ prepares. Accordingly, we refer to the place for the sacrament as a table.

Other Christian traditions have emphasized a different facet of the meaning of this event—the notion of the sacrament as a priestly participation in Christ's sacrificial offering on the cross. This interpretation focuses on Jesus' institution of the sacrament and subsequent death at the time of the Passover, and it highlights the idea of Christ as the Paschal Lamb given for the atonement of our sin. It can be related to the offerings of the temple and the writings of the early church (see Hebrews). In these traditions, the primary meaning of "Do this" has to do with offering the sacrifice, as the priest and the faithful together join in Christ's perpetual self-offering to God. Accordingly, these Christians refer to the place for the sacrament as an altar.

At the time of the Reformation, our theological ancestors asserted that the grace of God given to us through the death and resurrection of Jesus Christ is sufficient for all time and for all people. We are saved through faith alone, they insisted, and not as a result of any human action or merit. In particular, they made a strong critique of practices around the Catholic Mass that suggested the priestly actualization and mediation of God's saving work through the sacraments. By contrast, the Reformers understood the Lord's Supper as an act of thanksgiving and remembrance of what God had already done in Jesus Christ. For this reason, we have continued to think of the Lord's Supper primarily as a meal that Christ prepares for us, at which Christ presides—and the place for sharing this meal as a table.

Having said this, it should be noted that Reformed churches don't deny the idea of Jesus' self-offering for the forgiveness of sin, any more than other Christian traditions downplay the significance of eating and drinking with Christ. We may come to the table (or altar) from different places and with different histories and perspectives on the meaning of the sacrament, but there is one God who meets us there, one body of Christ in which we share, and one Spirit of truth who feeds us with mercy. By the grace of God, may we one day meet at the marriage supper of the Lamb. Perhaps this is what Jesus is calling us to do.

73   What things should be on the Communion table?

In many homes, level surfaces seem to have a magnetic power, attracting odd assortments of objects family members leave around—shopping bags, school books, stray socks, children's toys, and other clutter. When the clutter starts to encroach on the area available for plates and cups, it's a sign that, in all the business of daily life, we may be neglecting the primary purpose of the table—gathering for the family meal.

The same thing seems to be true in the church. It is common to see a brass standing cross, a pair of candles, a large Bible, and arrangements of flowers—among other things. The plate and cup for the Lord's Supper, if present at all, stand a good chance of getting lost in the crowd. What does this say about the primary purpose of the Lord's Table and the nature of our life together?

The church's table is, above all, a place for a meal—eating and drinking with the crucified and risen Lord. It is a place where the church "says grace," giving thanks for the great gift of God's saving love. It is a place for gathering as the family of faith, the body of Christ, and a place for renewing the bonds of our covenant relationship with God and one another. It is a place for nourishment in the Word through the power of the Spirit. And it is a place where we anticipate the great heavenly banquet to come, the wedding feast of heaven and earth.

Even where the Lord's Supper is not celebrated each week, keeping the plate and cup on the table can help us to remember the reason for this table: a place for communion in the body and blood of Christ. These things may even help to awaken our imagination to sacramental themes in the Scriptures and liturgy or whet our appetite for more frequent Communion.

The cross, the light, and the Bible are important symbols of our faith, and they deserve their own places of honor in the church. Consider finding an alternate location for the brass standing cross and candles—a high ledge or shallow table in the back of the chancel, perhaps. Or use a processional cross as a sign of the Lord who leads us in worship and service, and let the paschal candle stand alone as the primary symbol of the light of Christ. Instead of having the Bible on display on the Communion table, keep it on the lectern or pulpit where it will be used in worship. This placement will better convey our relationship to the Word of God—not a museum piece but a living source of wisdom and truth for the people of God.

10

Signs and Symbols

74 **What does "IHS" mean?**

The symbol *IHS* comes from the first three letters of "Jesus" in Greek: *iota* (*i*), *eta* (*h*), and *sigma* (*s*). In the ancient world, as in our own, abbreviated versions of proper names and other words were often generated by using the first few letters.

The fact that the Greek letter *eta* looks like an *h* in English has led to some creative interpretations of this symbol: *In Hoc Signo* ("In this sign" and "In his service") and *Iesus Hominem Salvator* (Jesus, savior of humanity). But these are all reverse acronyms—or "backronyms," if you will—false etymologies for this symbol, created after the fact. (Another well-known backronym is S.O.S., which was designed to be a simple and easily recognizable distress signal in Morse code; only later did people begin to use "Save our ship" or "Save our souls" as a mnemonic device for this pattern.)

There are other mysterious letters sometimes seen in our places of worship. The Greek letters *alpha* (*a*) and *omega* (looks like an upside-down *u*) together are a symbol of God "the first and last, the beginning and the end" (Rev. 22:12; see also Rev. 1:8 and 21:6). The Greek letters *chi* (*x*) and *rho* (*p*)—the first and second letters of the word "Christ" in Greek—are often combined to form the *chi-rho* symbol, which is reminiscent of a figure on a cross. The letters *INRI* stand for the Latin phrase *Iesus Nazarenus, Rex Iudaeorum*, or "Jesus of Nazareth, King of the Jews"; according to the Gospel of John, these words were inscribed in three languages (Hebrew, Latin, and Greek) on a sign above the cross on which

Jesus died (John 19:19–20). The symbol *ICXC*, seen most often in Eastern Orthodox iconography, is another way of abbreviating "Jesus Christ," using the first and last letters of each word in Greek (when it appears at the end of a word, the Greek letter *sigma* looks like a *c*).

Another ancient and familiar Christian symbol is that of the fish. The image of the fish may have been associated with Jesus' calling of fishers as disciples, his baptism with water, his feeding the multitude with a few loaves and fish, his resurrection meals in Luke and John, the "sign of Jonah" (Matt. 12:38–42), or all of the above. But early Christians also used the Greek word for fish, *ichthys*, as an acronym for the Greek phrase "Jesus Christ, God's Son, Savior" (*Iesous Christos, Theou Yios, Soter*)—a shorthand affirmation of faith.

What are the liturgical colors?

Well, all of the colors. According to Genesis, God put the whole rainbow in the clouds as a sign of the covenant with all flesh. Any color in God's creation can serve the church in glorifying our creator. But throughout the history of Christianity, certain colors have been used in particular ways. In its exhaustingly lavish description of the construction and adornment of the tabernacle, the book of Exodus mentions the use of blue, purple, crimson, and (sometimes) gold yarn no less than twenty-five times over the span of fifteen chapters (see Exod. 25–39).

For the first thousand years of Christian worship, apparently little thought was given to the use of liturgical colors. The white garments of baptism were standard-issue liturgical dress, with more elaborate vestments of various colors reserved for special occasions in the Christian year. In the medieval period, people began to experiment with the use of particular colors for seasons and festivals of the liturgical year, but these varied from region to region. It was only after 1570 in the Roman Catholic Church that standardized liturgical colors were introduced: white, red,

green, and violet, supplemented by black and rose on particular
occasions. Among Reformed Christians in the centuries that followed, Calvinists and Puritans tended to eschew liturgical colors
as well as the seasons they represented, preferring basic black. In
the past several decades, Reformed churches and other mainline
Protestants have come to embrace a schedule of liturgical colors
for the seasons and festivals of the Christian year. This relatively
recent development can be attributed to increased attention to (or
decreased suspicion of) the visual elements of Christian worship
as well as the successful marketing of liturgical supply catalogues.

The now-traditional liturgical colors more or less cover the
visible spectrum of the rainbow, along with the use of white and
no color (or sometimes black). White and gold are used for days
and seasons of particular joy and celebration—the Nativity of the
Lord, followed by the season of Christmas (including Epiphany),
and the Resurrection of the Lord, followed by the season of Easter
(including Ascension). Purple is used for the seasons of penitence
and preparation—Advent and Lent (including Ash Wednesday
and most of Holy Week); some communities use blue instead of
purple for Advent. Green is used in the time between seasons, or
ordinary time, when Sundays are marked in order. White (without
the gold) is also used for other festivals in ordinary time: Baptism,
Transfiguration, Trinity Sunday, All Saints' Day, and Christ the
King. Red is used on the Day of Pentecost and sometimes for
Palm/Passion Sunday and All Saints' Day.

During the liturgy of the Three Days, the liturgical colors
change in an especially dramatic way. Purple is used on Maundy
Thursday until the church is stripped at the conclusion of the service. The sanctuary remains bare through Good Friday, until it is
adorned with white and gold for the Easter Vigil. Other traditions
come into play for certain pastoral events—white is used at funerals and red may be used at services of ordination and installation or
at the dedication or anniversary of a church. At the celebration of
Baptism, Eucharist, or marriage the color of the season is retained.

While some have sought to attribute symbolic meanings to
the colors themselves (purple for royalty or green for growth, for
instance), the more important thing about liturgical colors is that

they help worshipers experience the seasons and festivals of the Christian year in a more vivid and dynamic way, engaging our imaginations and tinting time with meaning. The point isn't the colors themselves but how the colors point to what God has done, is doing, and will do in Jesus Christ.

76 What is the meaning of the big candle?

The paschal candle (or Easter candle) has a leading role in the Great Vigil of Easter, the first service of the Easter season and the grand drama at the height of the Christian year.

This service begins with the lighting of a "new fire," symbolizing Jesus' resurrection. The one whose life was utterly extinguished nevertheless rises from the ashes of death. Christ is the light that darkness could not overcome (John 1:5). The paschal candle is kindled from this new fire and used to light smaller candles held by worshipers. Even after those individual candles are extinguished at the conclusion of the Service of Light, the paschal candle is carried in procession throughout the Easter Vigil—through the Services of Readings, Baptism, and Eucharist.

In the context of the Great Vigil of Easter, the paschal candle has an array of symbolic associations, including the light God summoned at the dawn of creation (Gen. 1), the pillar of fire that led the people of Israel through the sea (Exod. 13–14), the image of Christ as the bright morning star (2 Pet. 1), and the light of the Lord illumining the new Jerusalem (Rev. 22). These biblical allusions are found in the *Exsultet* (or Easter Proclamation), an ancient hymn sung after the lighting of the paschal candle. Among other things, the *Exsultet* marvels at the way in which, like God's grace, the candle's light may be divided and shared without being diminished. In some versions, the *Exsultet* even gives thanks for the bees that provided the wax for the candle, an image linking the smallest of God's creatures with the great story of salvation.

The tradition of lighting a candle at the Easter Vigil probably had humble origins, beginning as an elaboration of the lighting of lamps for evening prayer. But as the paschal candle came to be a prominent symbol of Christ's resurrection, it grew in significance and stature, especially in the Middle Ages. The paschal candle at one English cathedral was said to be more than three stories tall.

In contemporary practice, a more modest paschal candle is the norm. Typically it is around three feet tall and is placed on a candle stand that brings it up to the height of an average person. It is often marked with a cross, the Greek letters *alpha* and *omega*, and numbers indicating the year. The paschal candle is used throughout the season of Easter, from the Great Vigil to the Day of Pentecost. We also light the paschal candle at baptisms and funerals, as it helps to illuminate our understanding of baptism as dying and rising with Christ and marks the funeral as a service of witness to the resurrection; at these services, the candle appropriately stands near the font or the coffin, respectively.

77 What is the significance of the various clerical garments?

Most liturgical vestments actually have their origins in the street clothes of an earlier era. The oldest and most basic is the alb (from the Latin *albus*, for "white"), a long white garment derived from the ancient Roman tunic. Early Christians received a bright, new alb at the time of their baptism. The alb has come to represent equality in ministry and can be worn by any baptized liturgical leader. The alb is sometimes worn with a simple rope belt called a cincture.

The Geneva gown is a black robe, once commonly worn in public by those with academic credentials. The Geneva gown symbolizes scholarly training and learned preaching, a historical value and strength of the Reformed tradition. The addition of three bars called chevrons to the sleeve signifies the doctoral degree. Bands or tabs—upside-down *V*-shaped collars—are magisterial insignia sometimes worn with the Geneva gown.

The poncho-like chasuble had its origins as a warm raincoat. In the Middle Ages, the chasuble came to be associated with the priestly administration of the Eucharist. Worn over the alb, the chasuble was elaborately and colorfully embroidered and was said to represent the yoke of Christ. Some in the Protestant/Reformed tradition feel that the chasuble conveys priestly pomp and privilege; others would argue that is a more appropriate garment for liturgical use than one displaying academic rank or suggesting judicial authority.

A stole is a long band of cloth, generally color coordinated with the liturgical season. Its practical origin was as a scarf, though it has come to be associated with ordained ministry and, like the chasuble, the yoke of service to Christ.

Continuing in the tradition of the Reformers, some pastors choose to wear contemporary street clothes to downplay the impression of clericalism and to emphasize the ministry of all believers. However, there are important considerations and potential risks here as well. Clothing can be a powerful cultural marker, as in the case of Scottish tartans, implying that the congregation has a particular and limited ethnic identity. Clothing often serves to accentuate gender roles and stereotypes, as is evident when worshipers feel compelled to comment on the wardrobes of women in ministry. Clothing may also convey economic status, as business attire may be associated with the power and privilege of certain professions.

Remember Paul's words to the Galatians: "As many of you as were baptized into Christ have clothed yourselves with Christ. There is no longer Jew or Greek, there is no longer slave or free, there is no longer male and female; for all of you are one in Christ Jesus" (Gal. 3:27–28). An advantage of the basic alb is that it signifies this sense of equality and mutuality among the people of God and underscores the good news of the gospel—that by the grace of God we are clothed in the righteousness of Christ.

78 Is it appropriate to have a flag in the sanctuary?

Churches sometimes choose to display an American flag in the sanctuary. There can be a variety of reasons for this choice: national pride, the value of engagement in civic life, support for military personnel or veterans, resolve to stand together in a time of crisis, or perhaps all of the above. But the decision to display the flag may also generate a variety of theological questions and concerns.

The Presbyterian/Reformed tradition has a strong emphasis on the sovereignty of God above all other powers and principalities. We believe that Jesus Christ alone is Lord. In a place of worship, a symbol of national sovereignty, such as a flag, presents a competing claim for our ultimate allegiance. Furthermore, we affirm our faith in the "one holy catholic and apostolic church" (Nicene Creed)—a church without national borders. The presence of a flag in the church undermines this universal affirmation. Things get especially problematic when a particular government supports or implements policies that may be contrary to the gospel.

Many churches that decide to display the flag try to address these theological concerns by using an additional banner—the so-called Christian flag. This flag, as common as it has become, was only introduced around a hundred years ago and is not recognized by other Christians around the world as a standard of the universal church. Indeed, it seems to be used almost exclusively within the United States, as revealed by its red, white, and blue color scheme—a design that complements the American flag.

In fact, we already have a strong and globally familiar symbol of the universal church in the form of the cross (see the following question). The presence of the cross in the sanctuary—whether hanging on a wall, found in the chancel, depicted on paraments, used in procession, or all of the above—is an unambiguous, unequivocal sign of the lordship of Jesus Christ and the sovereignty of the one triune God, "whom alone we worship and serve" (A Brief Statement of Faith, 10.1).

Congregations contemplating the addition or removal of a flag from the sanctuary might be well advised to study the Theological Declaration of Barmen, part of our *Book of Confessions*, written in 1934 by German church leaders in resistance to the rise of the Nazi party. Among other strong statements about the sovereignty of God, this document warns of the danger of "false doctrines" that conflate and confuse the authority of church and state (The Theological Declaration of Barmen, 8.22–24).

79 Should Presbyterian sanctuaries have a cross?

There is no specific instruction in the Presbyterian Church (U.S.A.) Directory for Worship on whether sanctuaries should or should not have a cross. Consequently, some Presbyterian churches have a cross in the sanctuary; others do not. The decision on whether to display a cross would be a matter for the church's session to determine (*Book of Order*, W-2.0303).

The Directory for Worship does, however, provide this important guidance on the place and purpose of such things in the sanctuary: "Certain prominent symbols from Scripture, such as light, book, water, bread, cup, and cross, play an important role in Christian worship. Such things are not objects to be worshiped, but signs that point to the grace of God in Jesus Christ" (W-1.0303). Any symbol in worship should serve the ultimate purpose of directing our attention and worship to God.

Typically, when a cross does appear in a Reformed/Presbyterian church, it is an empty cross—not depicting the figure of Jesus crucified. There are at least two good reasons for this.

First, the image of the empty cross reflects the primary setting for worship—the Lord's Day, the first day of the week, when Jesus rose from the dead. The empty cross is, in this sense, a "witness to the resurrection." It is a sign of the hope and joy of the gospel, the promise of new life that we celebrate each time we gather in the presence of our risen Lord. The symbol of an empty cross echoes the angel's message to the disciples on the day of Christ's resurrection: "'I know that you are looking for Jesus who was crucified. He is not here; for he has been raised'" (Matt. 28:6).

Second, the empty cross also says something about where we are in God's story of salvation—past, present, and future. In the words of the Apostles' Creed (note the verb tenses), we believe that Christ "*was* crucified, died, and *was* buried," but now "*is* seated at the right hand of the Father" and "*will* come again to judge the living and the dead" (italics added). With gratitude for the one who gave his life in love for the world, we now rejoice in the power of the risen Lord, even as we await his coming again in glory.

Glossary

Advent. Advent (meaning "arrival") is a season of preparation for Christmas and anticipation of Jesus' coming again. In current practice, it includes the four Sundays before December 25.

alb. A simple, white robe worn by worship leaders. Inspired by the new garment given at baptism in the early church, it represents the ministry and equality of all believers before God.

All Saints' Day. Observed on November 1 or an adjacent Sunday, All Saints' Day is an occasion to celebrate all the faithful people of God, particularly those who have died in the past year.

Alleluia. Hebrew ("Hallelujah"), by way of Latin, for "Praise the Lord." An expression of joyful praise especially associated with the season of Easter and used as a response to the blessing. In some traditions, alleluias are omitted in the season of Lent.

Amen. Hebrew for "Truly" or "Let it be so." A prayerful affirmation found throughout the Hebrew Scriptures, frequently spoken by Jesus ("Truly I tell you"), and used in the New Testament epistles and Revelation, this word has come to be a common response in Christian worship.

ascension. The Christian belief that Jesus now reigns in heaven at the right hand of God. Christ's ascension is celebrated on the sixth Thursday of Easter, forty days after his resurrection.

Ash Wednesday. A service marking the first day of Lent, in which the shape of the cross is drawn in ashes on worshipers' foreheads as a sign of repentance and mortality.

baptism. One of two sacraments in the PC(USA), baptism involves washing with water in the name of the triune God as a sign of our incorporation into the body of Christ. We remember Jesus' baptism by John in the Jordan on the first Sunday after Epiphany (January 6).

Benedictus. The song of Zechariah (Luke 1:68–79), often used in morning prayer. The Latin name comes from the first words: "Blessed [be the Lord God]."

blessing. An expression of favor. The blessing or benediction spoken by a minister at the end of worship is a proclamation of the grace, love, and communion of the triune God.

Book of Common Worship. A book of services and prayers for the PC(USA), first published in 1906. The most recent edition of the *BCW* was released in 2018.

Book of Confessions. Part 1 of the PC(USA) Constitution, containing documents from church history that express who we are, what we believe, and how we are called to live.

Book of Order. Part 2 of the PC(USA) Constitution, including the Foundations of Presbyterian Polity, the Form of Government, the Directory for Worship, and the Rules of Discipline.

canticle. A biblical song other than one of the psalms. Three canticles have special use in daily prayer: the songs of Mary (Luke 1), Zechariah (Luke 1), and Simeon (Luke 2).

catechism. A book of questions and answers for teaching the faith. Examples include the Heidelberg Catechism and the Shorter and Larger Westminster Catechisms.

charge. A call to faithfulness, spoken by a deacon, elder, or pastor as worshipers prepare to go forth in God's service. A charge may also refer to brief words of commissioning at ordinations.

chasuble. A liturgical garment, often colorfully designed and woven, worn in some traditions by the presider at the Eucharist or Lord's Supper.

Christ the King (or Reign of Christ). On the last Sunday before Advent, we proclaim Christ's sovereignty and celebrate the promise of his realm of righteousness, justice, and peace.

Christian year. Focused on events in the life of Jesus and the story of God's saving love through history, the Christian year (or liturgical calendar) helps the church keep time with Christ.

Christmas. A season for celebrating Jesus' incarnation and nativity, spanning the twelve days between December 25 (Nativity of the Lord) and January 6 (Epiphany of the Lord).

Communion. Sometimes used as a synonym for the Lord's Supper, Communion refers to intimate exchange with God and God's people, particularly through the sharing of the bread and cup.

confession. In Presbyterian worship, "confession" may refer to two things: (1) a prayer in which we acknowledge our sin before God or (2) an affirmation of faith from the *Book of Confessions.*

confirmation. Also called "Reaffirmation of Baptism upon Profession of Faith," confirmation is a time for those baptized as infants to affirm their faith and claim the promises of baptism.

daily prayer. Daily prayer offers a way to practice our faith at pivotal hours of the day (evening, night, morning, and midday). It involves psalms, Scripture reading, prayer, and other actions.

deacons. In the PC(USA), deacons are ordained to lead in the church's ministries of compassion, witness, and service. It is especially appropriate for deacons to read Scripture, lead prayer, prepare the Communion table, and offer the charge.

Directory for Worship. The authoritative guide to the theology and practice of worship in the PC(USA), found in the *Book of Order.* Its origin can be traced to the 1644 Westminster Directory for Worship.

doxology. An expression of praise to God, often sung or found at the conclusion of a prayer. The doxology is typically addressed to the three persons of the Trinity.

Easter. A season for celebrating Jesus' resurrection and ascension, spanning the fifty days (seven weeks, eight Sundays) from the Resurrection of the Lord to the Day of Pentecost.

Easter Vigil. On the eve of the Resurrection of the Lord, we celebrate the first service of Easter by bearing witness to the light of Christ, proclaiming the story of salvation, welcoming new members of Christ's body or reaffirming our baptism, and sharing a joyful feast in Jesus' name.

ecumenical. This word refers to the "one holy catholic and apostolic church" (Nicene Creed) throughout the world and to patterns of worship that seek to promote unity and reconciliation in Christ's body.

elders. In the PC(USA), (ruling) elders are ordained to lead in the church's ministries of discernment, governance, and nurture. It is especially appropriate for elders to read Scripture, lead prayer, serve Communion, and offer the charge.

Epiphany. On January 6, the last day of the season of Christmas, we celebrate the coming of Jesus Christ to redeem all people. The magi (Matt. 2) were the first to discover this good news.

Eucharist. Another word for the Sacrament of the Lord's Supper or Communion. "Eucharist" comes from a Greek word meaning thanksgiving, a central theme of the sacrament.

Exsultet. Latin for "[Let the heavenly host] exult." An ancient song of praise for the light of Christ used in connection with the paschal candle at the Easter Vigil.

festival. One of the major events ("feast days") of the Christian year, such as the Nativity of the Lord, Ash Wednesday, the Day of Pentecost, or All Saints' Day. Festivals may take place on Sunday (as in the Baptism or Resurrection of the Lord) or on other days of the week (such as Maundy Thursday or the Ascension of the Lord).

Geneva gown. A black robe sometimes worn by preachers in the Presbyterian/Reformed tradition. It is connected with the academic gown as a sign of scholarly training.

Gloria in Excelsis. Latin for "Glory in the highest." An ancient song of praise elaborating on the hymn of the heavenly host in Luke 2:14, often sung in response to the declaration of forgiveness.

Gloria Patri. Latin for "Glory to the Father." An ancient song of praise to the triune God, often sung at the reception of the offering.

Good Friday. On the final Friday in the season of Lent, we remember Jesus' suffering and death, join his prayer for the church and the world, and hear his anguished lament from the cross.

gospel. The good news of salvation through Jesus Christ. In lowercase, the word refers to the message in general; in uppercase, it refers to the books of Matthew, Mark, Luke, and John.

Great Thanksgiving. A prayer used in the sacrament of the Lord's Supper. It expresses gratitude for God's saving work, remembers Jesus Christ, and calls on the gift of the Holy Spirit.

Holy Week. The final week of the season of Lent, including Palm/Passion Sunday and the Three Days—Maundy Thursday, Good Friday, and the Easter Vigil.

Hosanna. Hebrew for "Save us" (see Ps. 118:25 and Matt. 21:9). This liturgical response is used especially on Palm/Passion Sunday and as part of the Sanctus sung in the Great Thanksgiving.

hymn. In its classic definition, a hymn is a song of praise to God. In common use, a hymn may refer to any song used in worship (including psalms and canticles), may encompass a range of themes (including confession, intercession, and lament), and may employ a variety of musical styles.

incarnation. The Christian doctrine of Jesus' coming into the world as God's Word made flesh. We celebrate this good news throughout the season of Christmas, every Sunday, and every night.

Kyrie Eleison. Greek for "Lord, have mercy." This liturgical response may be used in prayers of confession or intercession, expressing our yearning for God's grace.

lectionary. A set of Scripture readings appointed for particular days or times in worship.

Lent. Lent is a season of repentance, reconciliation, and spiritual renewal in preparation for the church's annual proclamation and celebration of the dying and rising of Jesus Christ. It spans the time between Ash Wednesday and Holy Saturday and includes forty days plus six Sundays.

liturgy. A pattern of worship or the prayers and actions therein. *Liturgy* comes from a Greek word meaning "public service" or "work of the people."

liturgical. Relating to the liturgy or concerning worship in general. Although some use this word to suggest a formal pattern of prayer, it can be used in reference to any form of worship.

Lord's Day. The celebration of Jesus' resurrection on the first day of the week. The Service for the Lord's Day provides for the proclamation of this good news in Word and sacrament.

Lord's Supper. One of two sacraments in the PC(USA), the Lord's Supper involves the sharing of the bread and cup in Jesus' name as a sign of our communion with God in the body of Christ.

Magnificat. The Song of Mary (Luke 1:46–55), often used in evening prayer and in Advent. The Latin name comes from the first word: "[My soul] magnifies [the Lord]."

Maundy Thursday. On the final Thursday in the season of Lent, we remember Christ's new commandment to love one another, wash feet in humble service, and share the Lord's Supper.

ministers of Word and Sacrament. In the PC(USA), ministers of Word and Sacrament (or pastors) are ordained to teach the faith and equip the saints for the work of ministry. Typically, the pastor as presider preaches the sermon and leads in the celebration of the sacraments.

mystery of faith. The death, resurrection, and promised return of Jesus Christ, celebrated in daily prayer and weekly worship throughout the Christian year and at baptisms and funerals.

nativity. The Christian doctrine of Jesus' birth as the firstborn of Mary and the only-begotten child of God. We celebrate this good news especially on December 25, the Nativity of the Lord.

Nunc Dimittis. The song of Simeon (Luke 2:29–32), often used in night prayer and at funerals. The Latin name comes from the first words: "Now you dismiss [your servant in peace]."

offering. In the broadest sense, this refers to the dedication of our lives to God, with gratitude for God's self-giving to us in Jesus Christ. In worship, it may refer to the collection of financial goods or the presentation of Communion elements as particular signs of our thanks and praise.

order of worship. A pattern of prayer and action for a service of worship. Orders of worship are important because, over time, they shape our lives as disciples of Jesus Christ.

ordinary time. One of two times in the Christian year (the time after Epiphany and the time after Pentecost) in which we are not observing a season but celebrating Sundays "in order."

ordination. The act of particular forms of service as deacons, elders, and pastors. Baptism is each Christian's primary ordination into service in Jesus' name.

Palm/Passion Sunday. At the beginning of Holy Week, on the sixth Sunday in Lent, we proclaim Jesus' triumphant entry into Jerusalem and remember his suffering and death on the cross.

parament. A piece of cloth, often in the liturgical color(s) of the season or festival, that hangs in front of the pulpit or over the Communion table.

paschal candle. A large candle symbolizing the light of Christ. It is used in the liturgy for the Great Vigil of Easter, throughout the season of Easter, and at baptisms and funerals.

Pentecost. On the last Sunday of Easter, we proclaim the gift of the Holy Spirit to Christ's church (see Acts 2) and celebrate the Spirit's gifts in our common life and ministry.

prayer for illumination. An important feature of Presbyterian worship, this prayer asks the Holy Spirit to empower the reading, hearing, proclaiming, understanding, and living of God's word.

Presbyterian. A denomination in the Reformed tradition. "Presbyterian" comes from a Greek word meaning elder, emphasizing the significance of elders in our form of government.

presider. A primary leader who guides the people through the service of worship. On the Lord's Day this is typically the pastor; in daily prayer it may be any member of the church.

psalm. One of 150 biblical songs in the Hebrew Scriptures. Christians use psalms in Lord's Day worship, in daily prayer, and as a "school of prayer" throughout our lives.

Reformed. A branch of the universal church originating among sixteenth-century Protestants in Europe, now spread throughout the world and including the PC(USA).

resurrection. The Christian doctrine of Jesus' rising from the dead on the first day of the week. We celebrate this good news throughout the season of Easter, every Sunday, and every morning.

Sabbath. The command to honor God by setting aside time for worship and rest. While some call Sunday the "Christian sabbath," the focus of the Lord's Day is God's new creation in Christ.

sacrament. A sign of the grace of God shared in Jesus Christ and celebrated in Christian worship. The PC(USA) recognizes two sacraments: baptism and the Lord's Supper.

Sanctus. Latin for "Holy." This ancient song is often sung as a response to the first part of the eucharistic prayer or Great Thanksgiving. It is an elaboration of the song of the seraphs in Isaiah 6:3 and also resembles the song of the four living creatures in Revelation 4:8.

season. A span of days in the Christian year, set aside for preparation and celebration of the central teachings of our faith—Advent, Christmas, Lent, and Easter.

Seder. The order of worship for the Jewish Passover meal. For reasons described in this book, Christian attempts to reconstruct or reenact Jesus' so-called last supper are problematic.

stole. A strip of cloth worn over the shoulders of a minister. Although it likely originated as a scarf, it now symbolizes a yoke—Christ's call to humble service and partnership in ministry.

Thanksgiving for Baptism. A prayer of gratitude for the gift of baptism. This form is used for the reaffirmation of baptism but not in the sacrament of baptism (i.e., when someone is baptized).

Thanksgiving over the Water. A prayer used in the sacrament of baptism. Like the Great Thanksgiving at the Lord's Supper, this prayer expresses gratitude for God's saving work, remembers Jesus Christ, and calls on the gift of the Holy Spirit.

theological. Relating to the content of our faith in God—what we believe. This book seeks to show how worship reveals and reflects our theology.

Three Days. The time from Maundy Thursday to the Resurrection of the Lord, including Good Friday and the Easter Vigil. The liturgy for the Three Days is one great service in three parts.

transfiguration. On the last Sunday before Lent, we remember the revelation of Jesus' divine glory to the disciples, in which his face shone like the sun.

Trinity Sunday. On the first Sunday after Pentecost, we proclaim the doctrine of the Trinity and celebrate the grace, love, and communion of the triune God.

Trinitarian (or triune). Relating to the Christian doctrine of the Trinity (one God in three persons) or describing a form of prayer that reflects our worship of the triune (three-in-one) God.

Trisagion. Greek for "Three times holy." This prayer for God's mercy has a threefold form and is often sung as a part of the Good Friday liturgy.

vestment. A special garment worn by worship leaders, such as an alb, robe, stole, or chasuble.

wholeness. Derived from the Hebrew concept of *shalom*, meaning peace, health, integrity, and well-being. A service of wholeness seeks God's promise of full and abundant life.

Word. In the Reformed tradition, this refers to (1) Jesus as God's Word made flesh, (2) the words of Scripture, and (3) the proclamation of the Word in worship and in daily life.

worship. From an old English word meaning "worth-ship," worship is the act of devoting ourselves to the one who is worthy of all honor, glory, and praise.